Fears of a Wantrepreneur

Christopher Grant

The Press at Grant Family Farm

Fears of a Wantrepreneur

This publication is designed to provide accurate and authoritative information with regard to the subject matter covered. It is sold with the understanding that the publisher is not engaged in rendering financial, accounting, or other professional advice. If financial advice or other expert assistance is required, the services of a competent professional should be sought.

Book Design by Unauthorized Media

Printed in the United States of America

First Printing, 2014

ISBN: 978-0-9914136-0-7

The Press at Grant Family Farm
P.O. Box 803
Essex MA 01929
www.fearsofawantrepreneur.com

This book is dedicated wholeheartedly to my best friend, egg washer extraordinaire, rock, and person, who believes in me even when I stop believing in myself.

To name names would be tacky…
But I call her "Mom."
-Chris

CONTENTS

Wantrepreneur

WANTREPRENEUR: an individual who wants to start a business, but has yet to begin

"Here's to the crazy ones. The rebels. The misfits. The troublemakers. The round pegs in the square holes. The ones who see things differently. They're not fond of rules, and they have no respect for the status quo. You can quote them, disagree with them, glorify or vilify them. About the only thing you can't do is ignore them. Because they change things. They push the human race forward. And while some may see them as the crazy ones, we see genius. Because the ones who are crazy enough to think that they can change the world, are the ones who do." – Steve Jobs, Entrepreneur

Here is the scary truth. If you work forty hours per week from age 25 to age 65, you will work roughly 83,200 hours. This is assuming you work five days a week, with some vacation time factored in. If you break it down, that is equal to about 9.5 years of your life. In reality, you will probably work some overtime and, in this day and age, it is unlikely you will retire completely at age 65. I will be conservative and call it 10 years.

10 years is a long time, especially in the prime of your life when you've only got about 60 years left. Here's a scary thought: wake up every day for the next forty years of your life and go to a job that you don't love. That idea has scared me since I was a child.

STARTING OUT

What should I be when I grow up? A teacher, a doctor, a lawyer? These jobs are highly specialized and require lots of education, including post-graduate degrees, and depending on how focused you are on a specialty, advanced training, for instance if you'd like to become not just a doctor, but a brain surgeon. I wasn't sure if I could master the necessary skills to have that kind of career. What if I did develop those skills and then found out it wasn't a good fit?

As I grew up, I learned that in order for me to be happy, I had to do it my way, and that meant having a job that I loved. I am one of the "crazy ones" that Steve Jobs referred to. I was the round peg in the square hole. And even today, I am the one who sees things a little differently. I am not fond of rules, and I have no respect for the status quo just because it is the status quo. Instead, I look for ways I can make the world around me function better, and often that means making the world different than it was before I decided to change it.

I have been like this since I was a little kid. While everyone else, who delivered newspapers, carried their newspapers in a one-strap bag that cut into their shoulder,

I attached three baskets to my bike. When I was asked to do something by a boss, I asked why. Not in terms of "Why do I have to do it?" but "Why are we doing this and not that?" When you work for other people, you always find things that you would do differently if you were running the show. But before you can run the show, there is an essential step you must take. So this book is not going to tell you how to become the next Steve Jobs, mainly because that has already been done. But you can model any number of entrepreneurs by doing something they all did once, twice, maybe even three times in their lives - they started.

What scares you? I'm serious, what in the world scares you? Think about when you were young. What were you scared of? You might have been scared of the dark, or maybe it was the monster under your bed. Because of that, your parents gave you a nightlight and checked under your bed to show that there was not a monster hiding there. Your parents were the first people to help you overcome the fears that once made your life scary. Today, wherever you are in your life, take a moment and really consider this question: What scares you?

The answer will probably be that there are many things that you fear. Some are obvious and others are tucked away in the back of your mind. Adult responses to the question, "What scares you?" includes things like snakes and spiders, heights, public speaking, death, and lack of money. Those things may scare you, but at the heart of the question remains the essence of the question itself: What is causing your fear? Failure, loneliness, ridicule, disappointment, pain, rejection? All these emotions do feed into our fears. But don't worry, this isn't one of those touchy-feely, sunshine-and-lollipop self-help books. Still we must face the fact that fear is something that everyone lives with all the time, and which stands between what we are doing, and what we want to do. Ultimately, it is fear that holds us back from accomplishing our goals, moving forward, or–most importantly– even starting. A new beginnings, a new starts, this for many people is the greatest fear of all.

And how do you conquer a fear? There are volumes of books that can tell you the scientific origins of fear in our brains, the biochemical flooding that takes place when we think about change and about all the imagined problems of beginning or starting something new. This is especially true in starting a new business because in business our fears are tied up with so many important aspects of our life. Our identity. Our money. Our social status. A very large part of our identity is tied to our work life.

How, then, can you conquer your fears when it comes to business? The first thing I can tell you is that you are not alone. Although it may seem like you are traveling uncharted territory, starting a business has been done every day, by many others for millenniums. Starting a business is, in fact, one of the basic building blocks of all societies and civilizations. The exchange of goods and services is truly the grease of our lives. Thus, a review of history would show entrepreneurs starting their business, after conquering their fears, just as in today's world entrepreneurs conquer their fears every day in order to start a new business. The fundamental step, in order to overcome any fear you have, is to recognize it, rationalize it, embrace it, and then keep pushing yourself forward. To be an entrepreneur, you have to think like an entrepreneur. And that starts now.

At its most basic level, the word "entrepreneur" is defined as someone who starts their own business. But there is much more to the word than just that. An entrepreneur has a dream. An entrepreneur takes risks. And because an entrepreneur is a person, the word entrepreneur encompasses all the messy, abstract, blurred-line elements that comprises each individual. I can't give you THE definition of an entrepreneur. I believe that the word is subject to circumstance and individual differences, and like most aspects of being human, there will be prevalent and less-prevalent aspects of the entrepreneurial personality. But there are some general features that I've found entrepreneurs have in common and that are ever present.

First, an entrepreneur is not your average, run-of-the-mill human being. He or she is a person, who doesn't just accept things the way they are handed to him or her, but is always looking at the situation and wondering why it is the way it is and whether there is a better way than the one currently being used. The entrepreneur is a person, who never stops learning, growing, and asking "why?" An entrepreneur is the kind of person, who goes the extra mile to not just achieve a goal, but to surpass it, and to make it the very best it can be. An entrepreneur is a person who makes something out of nothing. They are the people, who begin with the smallest seed of an idea in their mind, and start growing and feeding that idea because they know it can become something very real. And an entrepreneur is a person, who can follow his dreams sustained with the faith that entrepreneurs have, to see where those dreams lead and with the hope of the success those dreams will bring. These are the kind of people, who see an opportunity to make the world a better place, and then doesn't let it pass them by. They are the people, who see the "big picture," and understands how their little piece fits into it. They are the kind of people, who take the road less traveled to see where it leads them.

On this up-and-down ride that we call life, an entrepreneur is most of all a driver, not a passenger. While everyone else is just punching the clock and serving their time, entrepreneurs are the hands-on people, who take whatever life throws their way, bend and break as necessary, and use what they have to creatively to achieve a dream.

"Entrepreneurs are simply those who understand that there is little difference between obstacle and opportunity and are able to turn both to their advantage."
- Niccolo Machiavelli

I recently came across a LinkedIn profile description that read, "I am an aspiring entrepreneur; I would love to start a business." This made me wonder, what compelled the person to write that in their profile, but not actually do it? If you believe you have all the traits of an entrepreneur, but haven't taken the leap into starting a business, you are a potential entrepreneur. You may just be–what I call–a wantrepreneur - someone who has the dream, the potential, and the guts to start a business, but is waiting for "the right time" or "a sign." If that is the case, I really hope this book will be the sign you've been waiting for. I'll help you to take everything that might be a concern or a worry into consideration before you take the jump, but then I hope to give you that little nudge you need to get started. You may be standing on a cliff with your toes hanging over the edge. The first step is the scariest, and after you take that step, there will be plenty more fears to come. I hope my story will give you courage to keep moving forward. We've all felt the fear. But then we overcome that fear.

WANTREPRENEUR: a person who wants to start a business, but has yet to begin

So you have a big idea. You want to start a business. Congratulations! I wouldn't even know where to start if I wanted to find the statistics on how many people in the world thought they would one day like to start a business. It is a dream so many people have at one time or another. So many people sit in their cubicles at work dreaming and hoping that they can work for themselves, be the boss, answer to no one but themselves. But for the overwhelming majority of these people, the *dream* will forever remain just a dream. In fact, many people go through their lives crafting their business in their minds. They get stuck on the theory or the minute details and never get around to putting it into practice. They delay their dream, waiting for "the right time," "a better place financially" or "a sign." Well, here is your sign! You are reading this book Because you want to get started. You have the desire and–by seeking out information on starting a business, like this book–you show you have the motivation. Thus, the best way to start your business is by starting (see what I did there?).

I have presented workshops to high school groups about starting their own businesses. When asked why they might want to become their own boss, the first response is always "for the money." They also mention doing things differently, making their own schedule, and being powerful. These are all legitimate reasons, and they are all probably your reasons too, some more important and others less important. Soon, though, you find that excuses get in your way. And what many entrepreneurs have found is that one way to overcome these excuses is to set the groundwork for your business by putting your idea on paper. Jot down all the details about the business you want to start, as many as you can think of that come to mind. Will you need to hire an employee or two? Need office space? Licenses? Once you start, you'll be surprised at how, suddenly, your business, on paper, is becoming real.

And by the way, starting a business has nothing to do with age. If you think you are too young to start a business, you're wrong. In fact, in my experience, being young was one of the most profound keys to my success. Maybe I was naïve and just didn't know better than to think I could run my own business. Or, on the other hand, maybe I had the guts to go out and follow my dreams because when you are young, even if you fail, there is plenty of time to start again. But know this, at times you will ask yourself, "Why don't I just get a real job?" All entrepreneurs think that at one point or another.

We are conditioned to work for others because we have been told our entire lives that if we show up, sit in rows of desks, fill in the right bubbles with the correct pencil, and graduate, that we will become successful. Or at least we will meet the definition of what someone else, someone who has decided what their definition of "successful" is and decided that you, too, should live by their definition. There are some, and we all know these people, who believe that if we just shut up and go with the flow, we will move seamlessly through life unnoticed. Don't make waves, just swim with the current and you will be fine, they tell us. This philosophy is ingrained in us as little kids, when we want to be cool, to fit in. As little kids, we want to be part of the group. We go to great lengths to buy the right clothes, say the right things, and listen to the right music, all to fit in with a certain crowd. Our greatest fear is to not be a part of a crowd. To be alone is the great fear. And for most people, this behavior of "fitting in" is ingrained in them for the rest of their lives, and they will live their lives out in the world of the cubicle.

"Fitting in" is a weird concept to me, probably because I have never really fit in anywhere. Don't get me wrong, there is nothing wrong with fitting in. We all have to stop at stop signs, wait our turn in line at the store, and use our library card to check out books. But, there was a time in my life when I gave up trying to fit in. I stopped trying to please the "friends" that I thought I wanted and the groups that I thought I was drawn to. I had spent so much time trying to fit in, trying to figure out what other people wanted me to be, that I was being held back from doing the things that I really wanted to in high school, college, and even now at the beginning of my professional life.

You need to know that this isn't a book about a get-rich-quick idea, or some ineffective "ten steps to success" book with an "instant success" formula laid out for you. It is the true story about what happened when I finally stopped trying to fit in, forgot about what I lacked, and truly started focusing on what I was capable of, what I wanted, and the skills I do have that I could use to build a business. To sustain my momentum, I have used this simple thought since I started my first business when I was 16 years old: *Why fit in, when you can get so much further and have much more fun when you stand out?* To be an entrepreneur, you can't really be one of those people, who want to fit in with the masses. If you end up fitting in with the majority of society, you will just be another onlooker at the parade as life passes you by.

> *"Faith is taking the first step, even when you don't see the whole staircase."* – Dr. Martin Luther King, Jr.

This is one of those quotes you see on motivational posters, I know. And it is so popular because it is so very true. We fear the unknown, and we fear that we can't see the whole staircase, and our fear of starting is mainly about the future because we can't see it. When we work for someone else, the paycheck is already assured, and we just have to wait out the two weeks and suddenly, there it is. This reverberates with us because as human beings we like the security of knowing the end result even before we start. So many things are completely out of our control that the comfort of the "known" versus the "unknown" can keep us in our old pattern.

For example, when you go to an amusement park, before you get strapped into the roller coaster, you feel good knowing that all the riders, who came before you, arrived at the end of the ride safely. You feel secure knowing that there will be ups and downs, scary parts, and even risk (God forbid something was to go wrong) but, overall, the security is in the same pattern that others have experienced and been fine with. You see the ride start and stop at the same place. When it ends, you exit and the next group gets on. You get on the roller coaster because you can see the whole "staircase" that Dr. King talked about. You feel safe because you see not only the first step, but also the entire staircase and the end result, and judging by the faces of the people, who went before you, all will turn out fine. In business, the end is not in the same place as you started. However, this does not mean "the end" should be feared. As well, the reward of having a fun ride and a safe return to where you began, is not promised.

As a wantrepreneur, you have the plan, goals, and ideas, but the first step is the scariest. The first step may be just telling someone in your life, someone that you trust, that you have this idea, and that you are going to start a business. This is a big step because sometimes the best ideas are held in people's thoughts and dreams out of the fear that they will be called crazy or laughed at. We will address this fear later on. When you take the very first step to shape your business idea, you have to trust that the first step is worth it, but to also realize that there are many more steps that follow. Going from a wantrepreneur to an entrepreneur is a process that takes time and guts. I am six-feet-two-inches tall. When I walk up stairs, I can take two to three steps at a time because my legs are extremely long. When starting your business, one step at a time is the only way to do it because even though I can take two or three steps at a time on the stairs, we all have to go through the necessary steps to starting our business. Skipping steps can create problems later on. Of course, depending on your business, and your own talents, some steps may be able to be skipped but you'll need to evaluate that aspect of starting and building your business carefully as you go along.

And some people have already been entrepreneurs, but have forgotten...

Tap the breaks, for a moment. Many of you, reading this book, may have already been entrepreneurs at one point in your lives. You might be forgetting your lemonade stand from your childhood, your first ever, business venture. And if you ask a normal person what they do when life gives you lemons, I'm sure that they would respond "make lemonade." And if you see me on the street or in line at Dunkin Donuts and ask me that very question, "What do you do when life gives you lemons?" I will answer by saying, "I would make lemon squares, lemon meringue pie, lemon preserves, make lemon concentrate and freeze it until the lemonade market demands it, and then sell it to lemonade retailers." It is not a bad thing if you responded by saying "make lemonade." It's simply the normal, programmed response that we are taught from a young age. In fact we need those people to sell lemonade. The roadside lemonade stand industry is indeed progressive.

The first entrepreneurial endeavor for most of us, when children, is the lemonade stand. The process of convincing your parents to allow you to sit out on the side of the road with a table and a pitcher of lemonade (whether it is Crystal Lite or the real stuff) and wait for the first willing passerby to buy from you is exciting as a child. This is your first opportunity to set the price, collect money, and make change just like all those big businesses you visit while shopping with your parents. These eager lemonade entrepreneurs usually work in groups, as it's hard to run a lemonade stand by yourself. Often it will be the siblings working together, or your childhood friends, who live in your neighborhood. And they soon break down the lemonade business into various roles—just as in real life—like advertising, production, and sales.

One eccentric child will demand the roll of boss because they believe they know how to run things better than their peers. For a short time, the business thrives with children screaming "lemonade for sale," waving signs at cars, and hustling the letter carrier, first with cuteness then with guilt. But soon, the thrill of lemonade stand wears off faster than it came to be. You end up drinking all of your lemonade in order to avoid heat exhaustion, from baking out in the sun all day. Then the day will, likely, end as you close down the lemonade stand and place your bedazzled signs in the garage, with the card table sticky from lemon juice and sugar.

The memory lasts, but the business may never open again. This first stint in business is a great lesson for children. I am not sure of the statistics on roadside lemonade stand failure, but some do very well and some, not so well. My contact at the National Association of Roadside Lemonade Stands neglects to reveal the numbers behind the business failures and successes for lemonade stands.

Had you made some other product, instead of lemonade, the fate of your stand may have been different. You might have found new and amazing success with your lemon square endeavor, and later success beyond your wildest dreams, when you sold out to Entenmann's. But, for those of you who have sat in the sun and heat on a summer day, in an effort to sell lemonade or another product, you know this feeling all too well. When the fun dies down, often within the first day, your parents end up bringing in the abandoned card table. But even if the business didn't last, while reading this I am sure the memory of that day was brought back to you.

So with this in mind, I suggest that when someone says "when life gives you lemons," you respond like an entrepreneur just as I do, and say, "I would make lemon squares, lemon meringue pie, lemon preserves, make lemon concentrate and freeze it until the lemonade market demands it then sell it to lemonade retailers. Will you get a weird look? Yes. Will you get a sarcastic laugh? I hope so. If you aren't in the right company to be able to respond in a creative and entrepreneurial manner, then they are probably out of line in asking such a question, and you are definitely keeping the wrong company. So whatever you do, when life gives you lemons, take them, because there are very few things just given to you that are as sweet as lemons, once an entrepreneur turns them into a business!

And on another note, the next time you see a card table on the side of the road with a slew of kids waving signs around a pitcher of lemonade, pull over and buy a glass, not only for your refreshment, but for the spirit of the kids who are trying to learn the entrepreneurial way. Maybe your contribution of a quarter or two will help keep the entrepreneurial spirit alive for them and be the burgeoning seed of a business they will develop down the road, as they become adults.

And speaking of supporting the entrepreneurial spirit, it has come to my attention that some towns and cities are declaring war on these ambitious children. Claiming everything from health code violations, to operating without business permits, the effort to snuff out the entrepreneurial spirit of children should be considered a crime. The dreams of our children to work for themselves should be started early, and then sustained fervently. The people, who are responsible for this, are suffocating the dreams of children everywhere. That is why we could use an organization like The National Association of Roadside Lemonade Stands right here in the United States.

The idea of being given a situation that is not great, like being given lemons, and responding in the normal manner as most would, by making lemonade, can be translated into anything and everything that we do in life. Each day we are put into a wide range of situations, good and bad. How we react to them will dictate where your life goes. The focus of my story is about my journey in business, and how I respond to lemons, time and time again, from my first idea to where I am today. There is so much that you cannot control in this world, but one thing you can control is you, and how you react to every situation in life, whether the situation is good or not so good. When you take the first steps to becoming an entrepreneur, no matter how scary it may be, when life gives you lemons, you had better get moving and get creative and turn the sour to sweet and tasty.

WARNING

If you are looking for a 9-to-5 job, or already have one and are just fine with working in the cubicle, entrepreneurship probably isn't the way to go. Not that you have to work all 168 hours that comprise a week in order to live the entrepreneur life, but you will find that when you are a sole proprietor and your only employee is yourself, every minute of the day is valuable. If you have a dream of starting a business, but think it will just happen by itself, you're probably not going to get too far.

When I worked as an intern for another farmer, he told me something I will never forget. We were having one of those days when everything went wrong. I was breaking equipment left and right, he was getting tractors stuck in the mud, and a pop-up thunderstorm forced us home for the day. In the truck, he looked at me as he took off his soaking wet hat and said, "So you still wanna be a farmer right?" I said, "Yup." He laughed and said, "If it was easy, everyone would be doing it…and we wouldn't have jobs."

This is all too true, not just in agriculture, but in entrepreneurship as well. If starting and managing your own business was easy, everyone would be doing it. The world would be filled with sole proprietors and CEOs, and there would be no one to work for your business. It takes a different kind of person to start a business. It takes someone, who can roll with the punches, and get right back up to punch back. It takes someone with the ability to not only ride the roller coaster but also to be able to slow it down when it starts moving too fast, or get out and push when it's stuck. All this for the sake of achieving your dream and changing your life. All this to transform yourself from a wantrepreneur into an entrepreneur.

MY STORY

How do I know so much about the fears of a wantrepreneur? I've been there, and I am there, every day. When I was growing up, we were lucky to live on the farm where my dad worked. I grew up watching my dad do a job he loved, farming. My aunt, uncle, and three cousins, along with my parents, brother and sister, all live together in one of the most beautiful places in the world and we kids played outside, where kids belong. When the owner of the farm passed away, my parents and aunt and uncle were faced with a challenge. Where to go? The new owner of the property was not a farmer, and sold the farm off in lots. With luck on our side, between our two families, we were able to buy our house and a few acres of land. My father became a full-time firefighter. My mother went to work and runs a hardware store. My uncle works at another hardware store and my aunt became a full-time nurse. The farm and business were no more.

We had a two-family house, a barn, and a few chickens in the garden. I grew up working in the garden alongside my uncle Rick, and in the chicken coop with my dad. When I was 14, my garden had grown to the point where we couldn't eat every vegetable that came out of it. So when my parents were away for the weekend, I set up a roadside table, painted a sign that said "Vegetables" and formed my first business. I sold every vegetable I could bring down there, with people leaving their payments in a coffee can because it was all a trust-based business; they would take what they wanted and leave the money.

At that time, I had the only farmstand in town. Now there are two on my street. This was the first time I had made any money. It was only a few bucks a day, but it set me on the path toward growing my business (no pun intended). The roadside stand was phased out when I turned 16 and I started Grant's Plants, a wholesale perennial company, but more about that later. When I was 21, I formed Grant Family Farm. I grow vegetables, cut flowers, and eggs for local farmers, markets and a small CSA or community supported agriculture program. I use my family's land as the hub of the business. Most of my fields for growing crops are scattered around my small town, and are borrowed or rented from the land owners. When I say rent, I mean paid for with vegetables. The owners have their land farmed by me and in return receive fresh vegetables.

When people see me and my business, they assume that I am a multi-generation farmer taking over for my parents. In a way I am. I consider myself a 1.5 generation farmer. I started an agricultural business in a technology-oriented state. I started with no money, no formal business education, and no idea just how much work and fun I would have starting and running my own business. I haven't mentioned that much, so let me say here that being an entrepreneur is fun. Making the decisions is responsible but it is also fun. And that's pretty easy to understand. Psychology, for instance, uses a classification system, which is very well-known, and called Maslow's hierarchy. According to Maslow's hierarchy, once we have a roof over our heads, clothes on our back, and food in our belly, human beings are singularly motivated by what Maslow defined as "self-realization." It is self-realization that brings happiness. And being in control of our own destiny and being the decision maker and being creative as an entrepreneur fits all those qualities, and that is a happy state of being. I learned that in college of all places. Now that doesn't mean there aren't hard days, or days when everything goes wrong. But all in all, being an entrepreneur is fun even when it's work.

Entrepreneurship is, of course, a journey, not a destination. You have to be willing to throw your GPS out the window, follow your heart, trust your gut, and never stop growing. That's just what I did with every step I took down that less-traveled road, and with each piece of crop land I added to those I was farming. I stopped trying to fit in the box, found something I loved to do, believed in myself, and never made the mistake of thinking that I know everything about anything.

This is not written from the top of a mountain looking

down at the path that I took to greatness, like other books by millionaires or celebrity entrepreneurs. This book is written during the journey, based on my experiences navigating the business world without a business degree, money, or experience.

RISK

Starting a business does involve risk. Risk is exposing yourself to hurt, danger, or loss. If you take a risk by leaving your job to start your own business, you may be risking a lot. Depending on where in life you are, your obligations, and your situation, may make taking the entrepreneurial road to be a huge risk. You risk losing so much during the infancy of your business, as you struggle to get your dream off the ground. Taking this financial risk is one of the scariest thoughts for many wantrepreneurs. I don't know many people, who have a giant saving's cushion set aside so they can start their dream business. The absence of a steady paycheck might make your bank account and lifestyle sweat when times get tough. If I told you that I have never bounced a check in my career, I would be lying. Someone asked me how I was qualified to write a book on entrepreneurship when I've run out of money once or twice.

I like to think the answer is that it is all a part of the game. A part of the entrepreneurial experience to log on to your online banking site and see that you overdrew with the last check you wrote. No one is perfect. The financial risk will be whatever you make of it. When money is tight, that's when creativity comes in and needs to be put to work. Other risks of the entrepreneur include risking your relationships with others, who may not understand or support your dreams. I have been quoted saying that my longest relationship was with my Blackberry smart phone (although I believe my iPhone and I have another anniversary coming up). When you take on another responsibility like a business, you are going to want to spend every minute you can on the business. This is both a great thing and a horrible thing. Wanting to spend every moment working will lead you down the path where your relationships will suffer.

Your boyfriend or girlfriend, your spouse, your friends, and your family will all be affected as you spend more time with your business. Sounds weird I know, but it is true. The balance of meeting your personal obligations with your business obligations will be tough, but you will learn quickly when you are off balance and find a way to make it all work. Don't mistake the difference of making a living and not having any life outside of your business. Believe it or not, some entrepreneurs have fallen into the trap of working too much. I am guilty of that myself. When the going gets tough, work is the only way out, at least that is how entrepreneurs usually feel. I am notorious for burying myself in my work so I don't have to deal with "life." As exhausting as being an entrepreneur can be, many entrepreneurs find themselves unable to step away from their business for any period of time. This, for me, has lead to the loss of relationships, friendships, and a general drifting away from some of the people that I have known and been friends with. And it is this "balancing" of the entrepreneurial life and the personal life that is where I am still learning to balance my life with making a living.

> *"Risk more than others think is safe. Dream more than others think is practical."*
> — Howard Schultz

By becoming an entrepreneur, yes, you are risking money and relationships, but the biggest risk that looms overhead is the risk of failure. This is the personal, deeply emotional pain of the possible failure of your entrepreneurial business. I know, it is pretty obvious that you are risking looking like a failure if you make the wrong move, make bad decisions, or–ultimately–go out of business. This is scary because we care so much about looking like a failure to anyone we know, including our friends, family, and spouses. Entrepreneurs risk looking like a failure, in order to become a success. If you are so wrapped up in the fear that you will fail, you will never give yourself the chance to succeed. And in fact you may even create situations that will cause you to fail. But when you begin taking baby steps, the risks will be small and manageable, and you can incrementally grow your business and as your business grows, you'll learn how to be an entrepreneur, a step at a time.

Remember, we all take tiny risks every day: when we get

behind the wheel of a car, when we buy sushi at a gas station (never recommended:), or when we finally talk to the person we have been waiting to talk to. We take these risks because they are manageable. If you looked at the long list of risks that you will have to come face to face with when starting a business, you might want to puke. Save your breakfast, by taking each small risk one at a time.

"If you are not willing to risk the unusual, you will have to settle for the ordinary" — Jim Rohn

FEAR

"The oldest and strongest emotion of mankind is fear, and the oldest and strongest kind of fear is fear of the unknown." - H.P. Lovecraft

This quote sums up everything I want to impress upon you about fear. You have your dream business, and you want to make that dream a reality, but I know that you have a mountain of fear that stands in your way. The fear of failure, not being enough, bad timing, financial worries, what other people will think, distractions, mistakes, changing visions, and even failure. Yes, I said failure twice. These are all legitimate fears for a wantrepreneur. Your business is going to be your creation. You have the dream, but putting it into motion and breathing life into your enterprise won't be easy. All of those fears are legitimate, but none of them is so great that you should be discouraged from moving forward. You will deal with these same fears in other areas of your life wherever you go. As a wantrepreneur, these fears are magnified because your business will be part of you. It is your creation and you've taken a huge leap in order to start it. As the "boss," when something does go wrong, which it will, you can't run to the boss to fix it. You will be fixing it, whether the problem is big or small. You shouldn't fear that responsibility, but embrace it, because when you do start your own business, you will be the boss, and you'll be free to make your own decisions. And you may be surprised at how fast you learn to take control, manage your business well, and how much you enjoy being the boss and making the decisions.

> *"In order to succeed, your desire for success should be greater than your fear of failure."*
> — Bill Cosby

Why wouldn't you want to be your own boss?

I once asked a group of high schoolers why someone *wouldn't* want to start a business or be their own boss. Multiple students responded with answers along the lines of "they aren't smart enough." I was shocked. This was an answer I hadn't expected and I didn't really know what to say. As I was driving away, I had this thought though, "To be an entrepreneur, you don't need to be valedictorian of your class, you don't have to go to an Ivy League school, and you don't have to know everything."

And I'm going to drop a truth bomb on you right now. The majority of valedictorians, Ivy League grads, and geniuses aren't the ones who create. These people are all valuable to businesses and universities. They get hired to do jobs that they are well qualified for as a career, for an established business.

There are all kinds of "smarts" in the world. You cannot think less of yourself if you aren't particularly "book smart." I have trouble reading something in a book, or any kind of directions for that matter, and comprehending what I read, which isn't to say that books and the knowledge in them, just as with this book, isn't valuable. But, I am saying that if I can physically do something, that is when I learn. And that's true for most people, as we all learn best by doing. As to me? I am a hands-on learner. I am creative; I am analytical; and I am always asking questions because that is how I learn. The key to education is finding out how you learn and how you can seek out and then receive the information you need, and make it work for you.

If you set out to be just another "Joe Schmoe" business, that is OK. If you work hard and walk the same road other businesses have, you will likely find success, because of the fact that there are already companies out there that have done what you want to do, as the saying goes "the path's been trod," and you can follow that model, and there's nothing wrong with that. But if you want to make something different, travel a different road, and make your golden idea or your golden dream a reality, settling for ordinary or trying to fit in will only hold you back from truly standing out.

Who doesn't want to be their own boss?

The same group of high schoolers was great when I asked,

"Who wants to be their own boss?" Hands flew up, and I asked why. Everyone said, "For the money." OK, OK, OK, I get that, but what else are the perks of being your own boss? Flexibility, making decisions, people working for you, you don't have to answer to someone else? The list goes on and on. There are many perks of being your own boss, but there is also a lot of responsibility. You have to be a motivated self-starter (a term you only see when you look to apply for a job). Someone who will get up and go. There are many reasons to be sole proprietor or the boss, but money can't be the only one.

"Two roads diverge in a yellow wood,
And sorry I could not travel both
And be one traveler, long I stood."
— Robert Frost

Robert Frost wrote these lines in his famous work *The Road Not Taken*. The poem describes his walk through the woods. He comes to a fork where the path diverges. One path is obviously well-traveled. Many people before him had gone in that direction because it was safe, it followed the flow of the path they had started out on, and was the most likely path to lead to a worthwhile destination. The alternate path went off in a different direction. This trail had little wear, and had become overgrown and unwelcoming. This is a common occurrence for all of us when hiking trails in the woods and when following paths in life. We come to forks in our lives and we stand their looking at our options and trying to decide the best path to take.

No matter where you go or what you do in life, there are always going to be decisions that, once made, will dictate the direction your life will go. I know most aren't in the woods, or even on the road (thanks to GPS these days) but the decisions will be there, facing us, waiting for us to choose. Frost, in the poem, weighs his options. If he takes the well-traveled path, it will be easier and it may lead to something good. Yet at the same time, the journey and the destination have already been seen by many, and we know what choice has been made most often: the well-traveled path. The less-traveled path is intriguing, though.

Why, we might ask, would people avoid this adventure? By taking a less-traveled road, you may end up walking to a dead end or back around to where you started, but you might also see things few others have seen and do things few others have done. The well-beaten path might lead to a finite destination after a leisurely walk through the woods. But the road less-traveled might also take you to a place even better, even if you have to wade through overgrowth and cope with the fear that you may end up nowhere at all. The rewards might be spectacular. Frost finishes his poem by saying, "Two roads diverge in a yellow wood, and I – / I took the one less traveled by, / And that has made all the difference."

As an entrepreneur, you are making that decision. When the road splits off into many more than two directions, taking just another job or starting your own business are some of the options you will have. The well-traveled road is the one where you choose to work at a posted job. This isn't the easy road, but more so the well-traveled one. The less-traveled road, overgrown with obstacles, is the road of starting your own business. Instead of seeing the dark path ahead, see the adventure that you can tackle as an entrepreneur. The road is less-traveled not because the destination is not great, but because the risks you take to get there may be great. There is no guarantee you will even reach your destination. Take Robert Frost's and my advice: "I took the one less traveled by, / And that has made all the difference."

"When you cannot make up your mind which two evenly balanced courses of action you should take, choose the bolder."
— General W.J. Slim

SUCCESSFUL CAREER

As I express all the reasons you should start a business, I can't forget to tap the brakes and let you know that, although I love my career as an entrepreneur, it's not for everyone. I don't want to downplay the rewarding aspects of having a traditional career, which are there and which many find to be a good choice for them. In fact, not being an entrepreneur is far more popular than having your own business. There are a lot more employees in the world than there are entrepreneurs. I don't want you to feel that if you do work for another company, you will be miserable. I have the utmost respect for people who love their jobs. That is what it is all about. I know that having a traditional career can be just as challenging as being an entrepreneur in many ways. I hope that whatever you choose to do in your life, it is rewarding. I hope that you can wake up every morning and look forward to your day.

I'm not saying that you have to go skipping out the door with a smile from ear-to-ear, but I hope you enjoy what you do. A major part of life is finding out where you belong, who you belong with, and the career field in which you belong. I hope you find where you belong and that the choice you make brings you rewards. But since you are reading this book, you have something within that is telling you to work for yourself, or something that is nagging at you to, at least, consider working for yourself. And as I've said, it is the path less-traveled.

DREAM

We all have dreams, and not only when sleeping (because I am one of those weird people who doesn't remember what happens in my dreams when I sleep). The best dreams are the ones we see when awake and then choose to live. Our dream job or dream lives begin as figments in our minds formulated by ourselves. We all have a vision of where we want to be when we "grow up," the dream family, the dream house with our pets running around, and which is paid for with our dream job. The dreams we have and the visions we design in our minds change as we grow with our experiences and as we grow older. Our desires change with our values. So many things impede us from achieving our goals. Life gets complicated when you pull your head out of the clouds. The demands of daily life are tough. They take a toll on us and, more importantly, on our dreams. Many dreamers before us have failed to achieve their dreams because they had to compromise. Many people have made choices that took them down a path different from what they really wanted. For one reason or another, finances, family, or other obligations grew beyond their control.

You can look at your own life thus far, and easily remember something that you have compromised to make things easier. Maybe instead of going to the faraway college you dreamed of as a little kid, you chose to stay closer to home to save money. That's just one example of the small compromises that people make every day to keep moving forward. Each small concession you make, each compromise you allow, takes you down a different trajectory in your life, steering you away from your vision, until you end up somewhere completely different from where you intended. The life you dreamed of has turned into something you don't even recognize.

Half of my personality is made up of the dreamer and the other half of me is the severe realist. I know the phrase "life happens" and there are events and circumstances that are out of your control. Making decisions is one part of life that many people hate. Indecisiveness can become paralyzing, because people are so scared of making a mistake. For the sake of this, your life, and because you are reading this book which says a lot about what you want in life, I am asking you to dream.

Dream of the business you have held onto in the back of your mind. Building this vision of your storefront or your office and the people, who will work alongside you, is so exciting! I am also asking you to follow your dream and to take the steps that will make it happen. This book is all about the fears of a wantrepreneur, the person with the dream and the will to carry it out, but who is still holding back. There are many variables when it comes to starting a business, and with those variables comes a fear of the unknown. I hope these pages will help you replace the fear you have of starting a business with the faith in yourself to take that first step to achieve your dream with your whole heart and soul.

You have a big idea, huh? I am a big idea person, but I am also the kind of person who takes big ideas and puts them in motion (like this book). Growing up, my parents said that I could sell ice to a polar bear. I was always selling things. I had an eBay store in high school, selling anything and everything I could get my hands on. I sold things from our basement and the town dump to buy my first truck. Going back to my first farmstand, we lived on a busy street that was not a very safe street on which to stop. After my parents told me that I could not sell vegetables on the side of the road, I waited until they went away for the weekend and did it anyway. My business was born. My mindset, even when I was 13 years old, was that there were no farmstands in town. People need vegetables, so why not buy them from me?

"The value of an idea lies in the using of it."
—Thomas Edison

At 13 years old, I followed one of the most basic principles of business. I recognized a need and designed my business around filling that need.

Does your big idea, product, or service fill a need? Then

great! Take a deep look at your market. How different are you from the competition? Look through your phone book or do a Yelp search, or like most people these days, do a Google search for businesses like yours in the area. Look at the whole range of businesses that are in the realm of whatever product or service you would be offering. If you end up finding a company that does exactly what you were thinking of starting, don't panic. It's OK. This has happened before.

I had, what I thought was, a golden idea once. I always wondered why, when someone who had been looking for a job finally gets hired, someone close to them says, "Why didn't you say something?" because they knew someone hiring. During the recession, when I knew so many qualified people looking for jobs, I had the idea of starting a resume t-shirt company. A job seeker could go online, type the job title they wanted on the front in big, bold letters, such as "ACCOUNTANT," then type their resume on the back. They could wear the t-shirt in public and maybe run into someone, who was looking to hire an accountant. Bada bing! You found a job without even applying, saving the world from the recession. Cool idea, huh? It is such a good idea that when I Googled it, I found pages of companies that did just that in one way or another! (Go ahead and look it up.) My golden idea #4572 was a dud, not because someone else had already done it, but because I know nothing about the t-shirt business and didn't have a passion for resume writing. On another note, who in their right mind would wear their resume on a t-shirt?

There are so many businesses in the world that mirror their competitors, but still stand out for one reason or another. This is called their competitive advantage or their "thing." Even if a business is just like your golden idea, how can you stand out? There should be a long list of attributes your company can offer that make you better, in some aspect, than your competitors. My current business, selling farm products at farmers' markets, is the perfect opportunity to line up my competition, see what products they have to offer, and do the opposite or do it better than them.

What is the opposite of selling sweet corn? Selling bok choy of course! I scoped out each farmers' market where I sold vegetables, and created a spreadsheet of all the competitors and their products - everything from vegetables to cut flowers to eggs. If more than two people offered the same item, I did not grow it. This is easy to do when your competition is literally in the next tent. But in one way or another, you can map out your competition before you even put your business idea on paper. Research what works for them, and what you can improve on, to really focus on what will make you stand out. The online search engines have made this a much easier proposition than it once was. So, there is no excuse for a lack of substantial and detailed information on the area that interests you as an entrepreneur.

You have your golden idea! Bring it to life by writing it down on a piece of paper. Did you do it? I didn't think so, that is why I left this next page blank. Go ahead, write it down, and your idea doesn't even have to be in full sentences. It can be drawings for all I care! I will not be grading you and it is not a test score. My business, for instance, was started on a post-it note, which as we all know is a very, very small 3-inch-square piece of paper. But it served to create a concrete representation of what my being an entrepreneur meant, and that was all I needed to get started.

There you have it (hoping you wrote something). You've taken the first step toward starting your business.

"Begin, the rest is easy." - George Jenkins

Fears of a Wantrepreneur

If you have been thinking and dreaming of your business for years, I'm sure you have a pile of ideas stacking up, whether they are stacked in your brain or on post-it notes, and that these ideas are constantly changing. This quote really gets my rear in gear when I need to start something, big or small: *Just Begin*. With your business, it will always be a dream until you actually put it on paper. When you write down your goal, you are more likely to achieve it. When you create a concrete visualization of your idea by putting it on paper (or on a computer), you have taken the first step in starting your business. You took a blank sheet and wrote down or drew your idea or ideas for someone other than yourself to see. Or maybe just as a continuous visual reminder to yourself? Regardless, you have created a business in your mind and that means that, even if it is in the smallest way possible, you own a business.

You can then move further into your business idea, and add more and more ideas as you think of them. This doesn't have to be a formal business plan, but more of a constant "brain dump." By releasing all of the thoughts and ideas that crop up, or that you have been saving in that noggin of yours, and placing them on paper, you can have more room for new and original thoughts of what to do next in organizing your business on paper.

For the first five years of my business, I had no form of business plan. I was doing whatever the heck I wanted. I was being pulled in so many different directions that were not necessary and were a huge waste of time. When you have your dream on paper, you will be compelled to work toward it. Writing your dream down on paper will hold you accountable to it, because quite frankly, you created it. You own that business. You owe it a chance to come alive and be something other than just an idea. Your idea is just begging you to make it real.

CHRISTOPHER GRANT

HOMEWORK

If you have an idea for a business, I would not advise you to drop everything you are doing and go for it right this minute. Like any rational person, you should do your research. Most businesses are a result of research, which is then tempered through your own knowledge of the product or service you want to develop. Your business idea should be based on the simple process of recognizing a need and providing the product or service to fill that need. That is as simple as it can get. If your dream job is to own a fitness center, but there are ten others within walking distance already, something has to change. If you do have a dream of owning a gym, make sure you are in the right place for it. If the competition is steep in your area, that's one mountain you can overcome by recognizing a smaller subset of the population that goes to a gym.

Recognizing that there are all these people who belong to a gym, you should then ask yourself, what are they still not getting out of their membership? You know that, no matter if these people actually going to the gym or not, they are paying the membership fee. What is their experience lacking? If that is truly your dream, you will recognize at least a few aspects of the gym's culture that aren't being addressed. Maybe it is the atmosphere, the child care, or the judgmental nature of the people, who go to that particular gym and who make everyone else that attends the gym feel out of place. As a man who has never gone to a gym, I don't know, because that is not my passion. I could function on donuts and coffee for months at a time, and because of this it's clear that I would probably fail in the fitness industry. If you are familiar with an industry and know that your dream can fill a need you recognize, that is the first step.

What kind of resume should you have before you start a business?

There are no definitive criteria that you have to meet in order to start a business. If you want to open up a mechanic's shop and fix cars, but have never picked up a wrench, you will have to learn a lot. Your path will be less challenging if your business idea falls somewhere within your current skill set. Personally, I grew up raising vegetables and flowers. I have worked for large greenhouse growers, diversified vegetable farms, and even in the marketing department of a farm supply catalog. I have always worked within the industry of agriculture. Starting a business that is within my skill set gave me a head start. Working for someone else is a great way to learn how to or how not to run that business. By working for someone in the industry you'd like to be in, you'll pick up a lot of knowledge, while someone else is paying you to learn.

I have always been a questioner. I ask questions about everything, because I'm a curious person. While working for one greenhouse company, I wasn't very well liked by the owner because I often asked, "Why?" He thought I was asking, "Why me?" But the reason I asked questions was because I wanted to know how everything worked or fit into the big picture of the business. I learned a lot about my industry, how to run a business, and, even better, how not to run a business. You can look at a job in one of two ways. You can work to make money, or you can work to learn, taking every experience and using it to your advantage in your own business.

If you are dreaming about starting a business in an area in which you have little to no experience, you will have to learn. Don't be scared, learning is good. If I were to open a donut shop because I like donuts and see a need for a high-quality donut shop in my area, I would need to learn all about the donut industry, restaurant industry, and everything that makes up a donut business. Would it be easy? No, but if you are truly passionate about donuts, like I am, it will be a labor of love. I am not sure of any college that offers a Ph.D. in the donut sciences, so I would have to start teaching myself. The best way for me to learn is to find someone in the specific area whom I respect and buy them a cup of coffee. I ask for advice, direction, ideas, and encouragement. I am always talking with friends in the industry, and sometimes complete strangers. Even if your parents told you to never talk to strangers, now is your chance to break that rule, but please be careful.

Today information is limitless with the advent of the internet. You can learn anything by doing a simple Google search. The information on the internet is so vast that you can become an expert on practically anything in a short period of time, unlike the past when people had to learn by other means, like reading books. Books? I know, it's a crazy idea that at one point in time, you were only limited to the knowledge in a number of books in a library. If you are having trouble with a specific question, type it in a search engine and see what comes up, you have nothing to lose. You might find out that someone else had the same problem you did, and then wrote an article about it. You never know what is out there, and whether they are actually an authority on the subject, so take all the information you find with a grain of salt. Along with all the great information on the internet, there is also trash that someone vomited out there for the world to see. Contrary to popular belief, not everything you read on the internet is true.

If you want to thrive in business, take time to network and learn from those who are already doing so. If you are a cookie entrepreneur then you should read about Famous Amos and how he sold $300,000 worth of his cookies in his first year, and that was way back in 1975. And if you want to know how Famous Amos got to be so famous, you will have to work hard to track him down, because he is a busy man. Or you could read his book *The Famous Amos Story* or you can visit the website famous-amos.com. There is a lot of information available to you no matter what area of business you would like to be an entrepreneur in. So take advantage of all of them.

Everyone is busy these days, but most people enjoy talking about their business, and if you approach them properly they can and will often make time to help. How do you get to talk to someone you don't really know or who doesn't know you? That's easy. If you know of someone in your industry that you admire, write them an email or a letter, call on the phone, or ask them face to face. Just say, "Hi, I'm Chris Grant. I really like how you run your farmstand. Do you think I could stop in sometime and you could show me around?" It's that easy.

You don't have to flatter them with how much you love them and throw in facts that you found when you Googled them. Just be polite and appreciative of their time. If they ask how long it will take, shoot for 20 minutes. 20 minutes is just long enough to make an impression and get a good conversation going. Saying 30 minutes sounds like a long time, and 10 minutes isn't enough time to do much. When you stop in or meet with the person, or even if you just talk on the phone, ask realistic questions (not how much money do they make). Don't make it about you. Make sure you thank them, and when you are finished speaking with them, even follow-up with a quick email or note.

Why would anyone take the time out of their busy schedule to meet with you? If the person you are hoping to talk with loves what they do, they will care enough about the future of their industry and will want to get new people involved. People are always willing to help students or young people with ambition who are genuinely interested in what they do. If you are older and wanting a career change, they might still want to show off just how much they love their job and business, and would want to help any way they can. It's also a natural human characteristic to share. Most people love to share their knowledge and will readily give you at least a small amount of their time.

What if they don't want to talk?

If you try to get a dialogue going with someone you don't know and they say no, that is fine. If the owner is too busy, ask for someone else. If I were looking for insight on agri-tourism and the owner of the farm was too busy to meet me, I would ask for the manager in charge of the agri-tourism department. Persistence will pay off.

Take note, though, that this approach will not work if you are starting a competing business. If you walk into a meeting with Famous Amos himself and tell him you want to start a national cookie brand, he might not be too open to helping you achieve your dream. But since he sold his company to a large, brand-name company, he might feel that he is not constrained by the idea of competition. And, of course, if you meet with him and let him know you want to sell vegan cookies, however, he might have some good ideas for you. This all plays into networking yourself and your business.

For my first business, I grew perennial ground cover for garden centers. This was not exactly my idea. The business idea and supplies were given to me by my high school assistant principal. He and his family had once grown these plants to sell wholesale, and when he shut down, I picked up where he left off. I worked hard to produce plants that were high quality, just as his were. I found two garden centers that would buy them, just like they used to buy from him. The business was great, huh? He had everything figured out right? Not exactly.

The customers were doing a professional courtesy to my assistant principal by coming to me. The first year after he shut down, they began sourcing these plants from another much larger grower, until I came along. Then they began buying my plants at a slightly higher price than the other supplier, because I was local, and, well, I was young and adorable. I was trying to fill a demand that had already been met by a much larger company. I attempted to set myself apart with marketing and planting instructions, but the businesses and customers were non-responsive.

I spent 5 years on these products, trying to make them exciting, but I determined that perennial ground cover just isn't that exciting. The other thing that made that work so hard was that my heart wasn't in it. My heart didn't start racing when I talked about pachysandra or vinca. If anything, I would bore myself to death. Perennial ground cover is not my passion. Maybe someday I will have a burning desire to restart the business, but this is not that day.

As you see both of my businesses have been in agriculture, growing things for people. Working in the business of growing plants was a hands-on approach to market research. In the field of vegetable production, there are many avenues that a vegetable grower can follow, not only in regard to growing the products, but also marketing them. I worked with several vegetable growers, and as much as I wanted to become a big farmer, I learned that wholesaling produce is no way to get your feet wet in the business. I learned quickly that retail was the way to go. In my decision to retail my produce I had to determine where to sell it. All this had to happen before I ever put a seed in the ground. I had to weed through all of the obstacles that came my way, in order to get to where I wanted to be, running my business.

Almost everyone eats vegetables, yet in America, fewer and fewer people are growing them as a profession. It is said that less than 2% of the population of the United States is involved in production agriculture, and even fewer are involved in vegetable production. When I started out selling vegetables, I always thought to myself, "Who wouldn't buy vegetables from me?" when the real question should have been, "Who in their right mind would buy vegetables from me?" When you start selling your product, I'm sure you will have that exact notion, "Why wouldn't people buy mine?" More importantly, you should know every reason why anyone *would* give you the time of day to buy your product or service. Making a list of these the reasons will give you a great handle on where you stand. If you own a landscaping company, and the only reason you can think that a person would hire you is that you give free estimates, no one will hire you. Here is a tip: no one should ever pay for a work estimate like that.

I wanted to sell my produce at farmers' markets, so what did I do? I went to farmers' markets - a ton of them. I didn't wear my John Deere hat or work boots though. I went undercover, in "normal people" clothes. Too bad most of the vendors recognized me or knew who I was. I would go to these markets, sit, and watch. I looked at what the vendors brought, and took note of their pricing, staffing, and presentation. Then I would watch the people.

I come from a long line of professional people watchers. My mother is always watching people. But that's why we love her. I would observe how people bought their food, whether they brought bags, how they picked tomatoes and smelled them to see if they were good, and how people interacted with the staff at each booth. I had pages of notes about what to do, but more importantly what not to do. My biggest lessons were learned about the presentation of the booths. Vendors with the cleanest, warmest, and most well-presented booths attracted even those who weren't there to shop.

Applications for farmers' markets come out around the first of the year. These are just simple forms that you use to convey your contact information, what you will bring, and how much space you need. Most people think that farmers and other vendors just show up and sell, but that's not the case. Farmers' markets are operated by mostly volunteer groups that select the vendors and where they will go. In Massachusetts, farmers' markets are quite competitive to get into. I applied to six farmers' markets my first year. One after another, I received emails or letters notifying me that they were full and that I should try again next year. All but one rejected me - even the Cape Ann Farmers' Market, and I live and farm on Cape Ann!

I was accepted to the Salem Farmers' Market, one that I hadn't visited many times the previous year. I was accepted with the stipulation that I would not bring certain items, including corn, tomatoes, summer squash, zucchini, carrots, and beets. Taking to the woman on the phone, I was kind of upset asking her which items I *could* bring. I knew I would have to grow different items for this market, but never would I have thought that certain items would be banned. I was to grow bok choy, kohlrabi, lettuce, greens, kale, beans, cherry tomatoes, heirloom tomatoes, radishes, edamame, turnips, and flowers.

After my first few weeks at the Salem Farmers' Market, it finally hit me. All the other vendors had…well, the same products. Everyone else had corn, tomatoes, summer squash, zucchini, carrots, and beets. If I had brought those items, I would have failed before I even started because there was truly no more demand for them. I learned quickly that when your competition is literally right next to you, as with farmers' markets, the only way you can succeed is to stand out and fill the needs as they are presented.

Had I not grown unique items and evolved with the markets, I wouldn't have made it through the first year. Today, I focus on doing three new items per year for the markets as I see the demand. This was a hard lesson for a 20-year-old to learn. All I wanted was to be a vegetable farmer, but I realized that in order for me to do that and live my dream, I couldn't just raise the crops I like to grow and eat. I needed to grow what my customers like. I now sell hundreds of bunches of kale a week, something that I would not be doing if I grew only what I liked. As you may recall, I'm more of a donut guy than a kale guy, but I am learning.

What is so special about the Salem Farmers' Market?

The Salem Farmers' Market is special to me for many reasons. This was the first market to take a chance on me - a young, almost unknown business - and accept me into their very successful market. But there is more to this story.

Both my mother and my father were born and raised in the city of Salem, Massachusetts (yes, the witch trials city). When I was officially accepted into the market, to be held on Thursdays at Derby Square, I told my grandmother, who was living just minutes from the brick square. She was ecstatic, not because I would be seeing her every Thursday, but because of my great-grandfather. She told me that my great-grandfather, her father-in-law, used to sell his vegetables at the public market, right where I would be. Silas Warren Grant would rise at three in the morning to load his vegetables into his donkey-drawn wagon and drive from Hamilton to Salem to sell them. My grandmother always remembered him telling this story of the first job he had before enlisting in the Army and then working in manufacturing for the rest of his career.

My grandmother showed me a ring that had been in my grandfather's jewelry box. It is a gold band with a black onyx setting and the seal of the American Legion in the center. The date engraved inside is December 9, 1919, the day the American Legion was founded. It is an organization Silas loved and even helped establish with a post in Hamilton, Massachusetts. My grandmother gave it to me to wear at the farmers' market for good luck. The ring fit perfectly, never needing alteration to fit my finger. To this day, I have worn it at every farmers' market I have ever worked. I started wearing the ring other times too - farm meetings, when I traveled, and whenever I would step out of my comfort zone. The ring is my little piece of hope I can take with me, as a connection to my family history.

My grandmother loved seeing me wear the ring. Maybe it was because wearing jewelry is so foreign to me, but I think it was because she was proud of the fact that I am repeating history, and she had been a part of it. To think, over 100 years after Silas had been there, I would be back selling vegetables at the very same market. This time, however, the market opens at three in the afternoon and I've traded the donkey and wagon for a Chevy S-10.

When we first told her about my spot at the farmers market, she said that she would come and visit. Her visiting meant coming every week, through rain and the heat. I loved having her with me. She would set in that chair and polish tomatoes, and get us water when we ran out. During the low parts of the market, I would crouch down beside her chair, and I would look her in the eyes and ask, "So, what do you think?" She would always respond, "I don't, I don't get paid to think." I would hold her hand and talk about school, what I would have to pick and bring for next week, and pretty much anything that came to mind. She would stand next to me behind the display and hold onto my shoulder to watch the crowd pass by. The Salem Farmers' Market isn't just another place to sell vegetables. It is where I got my start, 100 years after my great-grandfather got his on the same brick square. Moments like this really made me feel like this was meant to be, no matter how hard it was to make it work.

My experience with the farmers' market is an example of recognizing needs in your industry. Your business will evolve from where it started and the need you initially filled. Doing your homework and researching your dream won't take just a few hours, but more like months or years, although if you want to spend the money you might reduce your learning curve with the help of a market research professional. Still, your grassroots research - learning from an employer, joining gyms, or shopping at potential competitors' establishments - will give you vast insight into what the norm is and how to break the mold. By doing so, you'll be able to do your business differently, and to make peoples' lives better.

By doing your homework and research, some of your fears will fade away as you become more prepared. Never forget that knowledge really is power.

SIDE BUSINESS

Are you the kind of person who does a cannonball right into the pool, or the kind who slowly inches in? I am the cannonball kind when it comes to pools, but the inching kind when it comes to business. When I started my business, I was 16 years old, and it was alongside other various jobs I held. It was a way to test the waters, if you will. I was not in a position to tell my employer, "Take a hike," because I needed the additional income to fund my side business. This can be a comfortable approach for someone offering a service-based business or goods that don't require a large investment. I know many farmers, who only sell at farmers' markets, myself included, because it is relatively inexpensive. When accepted, you need a tent, tables, a vehicle to get there, and product. Unlike farmstands that have to be staffed all week long and have product constantly flowing, farmers' markets are held weekly. The fee for setting up is anywhere from $20 to $30 each week. This system works for me and my business.

Ecommerce is one type of side business that offers great opportunity for entrepreneurs. Selling goods and services via the internet can really get you into business on a part-time basis, but it is increasingly competitive.

Many successful businesses have been started by weekend warriors - people who only work on the weekend. Whatever business you choose to start on the side, before you jump off the life raft of your "real job," you will have to make time to do what you love.

Side businesses are incredibly valuable when it comes to learning the ins and outs of running a business. Side businesses can be formed out of necessity, like the need for additional income for your family. I know many successful entrepreneurs, who have a side business along with their full-time career. The side business is common to people like hair dressers, mechanics, carpenters, and people, who have skills that can be used after normal business hours. Many of my own friends in these fields will do side jobs for extra money and to help people out. The side business is a great learning experience before you get a storefront or garage, to see if you have the demand to support yourself and the infrastructure of an entire business.

I will warn you that, in some careers, if an employer discovers you are running a side business they may see as competition, and you may find yourself in some hot water. If you start taking customers from them or if you are not focused on the task at hand when working for them, things may start to change. Be careful in this situation.

A side business will help get your feet wet and give you

an insight into running a business without going all in. This experience could give you the sign that you are not exactly ready to put all of your chips in the game, and you have to rethink your plan.

SIDE JOBS

Side businesses are an important way to test the waters before jumping in. They help you find out whether you want to be an entrepreneur, while making some extra money. For seasonal business entrepreneurs like me, the side job can be flipped. I am not an employee working on the side for my own business anymore. I am an entrepreneur that works on the side for someone else. This is a shift that you may experience yourself at some point. I love being able to run my farm, but I also love working for my friend, running a hydroponic farm part-time. This allows me to have extra income in the busy season, but also some income in the slow season.

Each situation is different. When you are an entrepreneur, you will quickly learn that knowing where the next check is coming from is critical. I have a side job that allows me to work year-round and still have some form of income, and I love it. I treat the hydroponic farm like it is my own and I get to solve problems, be creative, and make my own schedule. It's like being an entrepreneur for someone else's business.

MENTAL

As I write this, I am tempted to open a snap chat from a cute girl…if I had wi-fi, I would be on Facebook, and if I had any cash on me I would be at the movies. As a twenty-something, there are so many distractions that are present throughout the day that could keep me from, you know, getting work done. I feel they should re-coin the phrase "smart phone" to "dumb phone," because that is exactly what it is, a distraction that makes me dumb. When I was 16, there were even more distractions. There are so many things that will throw a wantrepreneur off track in this world!

I am a firm believer that you are only as good as the people with whom you surround yourself. If you want to be successful, you need to surround yourself with like-minded successful people. I know that you can look at your different subsets of friends and differentiate the doers from the…well, non-doers. There are those ambitious people, who grab the wheel and make their lives great, and then there are others, who are just along for the ride or even watching the bus go by. If you think about them for just a second you can place your friends into those three groups. I am a floater when it comes to friends.

I have a lot of friends, but no really best friends. I like being able to hang out with anyone when time allows. I can tell that I am more productive and driven when I surround myself with like-minded people. If I want to take a break, I enjoy time with people who are kind of along for the ride. The people with whom you surround yourself can really alter your mood. If you surround yourself with negative people, you will fall into a slump of negativity. I know that because I can see the impact it has on my business.

"Confidence is contagious, so is lack of confidence." – Michael O'Brien

I was running my business while going to the University of Massachusetts at Amherst. Most kids know it as "ZooMass," for being such a party school. I went to college for a reason, and my goal was to graduate. My parents never went to college. I am the youngest of three children, following a sister with bachelor's degree in psychology, a bachelor's degree in elementary education and master's degrees in special education, and a brother with an associate's degree in motor sports technology. I was there to get a piece of paper that would propel me further in life, not to drink myself blind Thursday night through Sunday morning. (This very section was typed in my dorm room, right after my roommate was carried in by two girls from another floor.) One of the biggest keys to my success is that I didn't drink until my 21st birthday. I know…not your typical college student. From then on, I would go out and have a good time, but I've always been aware of not getting too distracted with it.

These distractions, which are considered by many to be the "college experience," weren't really my distraction, because I had something more important - my business. I know I wasn't your normal UMass student, but I like to think that it has paid off. I enjoyed college, but not so much that I would lose my scholarships, business, or degree.

Drugs and alcohol are two major distractions, without which wantrepreneurs can do so much more. You will be hard pressed to find a successful entrepreneur, who will tell you that the key to success is a healthy diet of crack cocaine breakfast and celebratory Jim Beam throughout the day. That is all I will say about that. I'm getting off my soapbox now.

"Surround yourself with the right people, and realize your own worth. Honestly. There are enough bad people in the world – you don't need to be your own worst enemy."
– Lucy Hale

Go ahead and join a group for entrepreneurs, or seek out industry-specific programs for young entrepreneurs. This will give you a bank of information that you can use for the rest of your career. Networking will bring notice not only to your business, but also to yourself as an entrepreneur. At first, you will be the newbie. You may have to approach new groups of people and be the one to break the ice. There will also be a day when people come to you with thoughts on which they want feedback, and they will seek you out for advice. That will be a heartwarming day, and one that will make you feel great.

As you are preparing to go from a wantrepreneur to an entrepreneur, you should really surround yourself with good people who make you better, not bring you down. If you want your business to get off the ground, you may have to limit your distractions. I myself have yet to open the snapchat, but will when I finish this page.

TIMING

Timing, like location, is everything. We are all the same when we are waiting for the perfect time to do things. We wait for the right time to ask out a girl or guy, to buy our first car, and even to pay our bills between paychecks. Here is something I've learned about timing:

If you are waiting for the perfect time to do anything, you'll probably never do anything.

We make up excuses for postponing the start of a business. We cite obligations such as family, friends, other job, finances, and anything else that can come up. I am not recommending you tell your family, friends, job, and finances to kiss the curb. I just hope that you weigh your options out well enough that you take this all into consideration.

Like I said, I manage a hydroponic farm for a family friend, and love it. I have always had another job alongside my farm, for a few reasons. I like a challenge, and it helps me pay down my student loan debt. A second job that is flexible and enjoyable for me makes it feel like I'm not really working at all, although this is coming from a bachelor. My friends and family call my second job, which is less than 30 hours a week, my "real job."

It's true that balancing two or more jobs can become a juggling act, and it's likely the timing will never be perfect on all fronts. I always return to the idea that life happens. I know that no matter how much you plan for something, life will happen and you will have to live it on its own terms. As I am writing this book, I am dodging text messages about going out to dinner, because I have reserved this time for my "book work." With life happening all the time, carving out space to achieve your goals, and ultimately, your happiness is so important.

I would never tell you to quit your job; I know that is a complex situation all on its own.

It is scary when you finally start your business, when you actually let go of that "life raft" that is your other job. When you talk with other entrepreneurs, you will learn that they didn't just walk into their place of work one day and tell their boss they were quitting. As you start your business you will have to get creative about gradually lessening your responsibilities at your "real job," maybe transitioning to part-time if you can afford it. This advice does not apply if you are starting a competing business, but if you are open with your employer and let them know that your attention is required elsewhere, maybe they will work with you. With the other farmers I've worked with, they knew at the onset I had a business that would require flexibility. I hope you can strike a balance with your current business, or find employment that will allow flexibility and the income you need, while you are transforming yourself from a wantrepreneur to an entrepreneur.

"Do not wait until conditions are perfect to begin. Beginning makes the conditions perfect." — Alan Cohen

Making time for family, friends, church, and everything else that goes on in your day-to-day life will be a challenge, don't get me wrong. Everyone knows that with my seasonal business, you can't call me in the middle of planting season to go away for the weekend. They understand that in my business I have four to five months to make all my income for the year. That time is valuable, and also weather dependent. I am available all winter, though! When I first started my business in high school, besides scheduling school and another job, I set aside one hour at a time to work on "my job." All my ideas and thoughts that came up outside that time were written down and saved for later, so I wasn't wasting energy meant for school. These small chunks of time got the ball rolling slowly. I have managed to really take control of myself and my time with a calendar. Although during the growing season I don't always write everything I need to on the calendar, I do set aside time to do the things that are important to me. I am not equipped to write a book on time management, but it is crucial to starting and running a business successfully.

There are so many reasons why a person would start a business. Some people are tired of their job, and can see no other way out than starting a side business to get ahead. The loss of a job is a common time when people make a go of entrepreneurship, because they have nothing to lose. Today, when many people maintain multiple jobs to boost income, they are turning to home businesses and part-time ventures. Entrepreneurs are born out of passion, necessity, and drive. When I was 16, I had nothing to lose except the few hundred dollars I had saved. I had nothing, so I had nothing to lose, but I saw an opportunity and I went for it. Whatever makes your light go on and spurs your entrepreneurial spirit, grab it. Run with it. There is only so much time in your life to do what you truly love. There is no single way that people become entrepreneurs. Some people fall into entrepreneurship out of necessity. Some people find themselves halfway up the wrong ladder, but are scared to be at the bottom of the right one.

Waiting for the perfect time to do anything is, like I said, almost impossible. If you are waiting for your dream to fall out of the sky, packaged neatly in a box with directions, that will not be happening anytime soon, but good luck.

"If opportunity doesn't knock, build a door."
— Milton Berle

If you are waiting for the opportunity to follow your dream, it may not show up printed on a billboard. For some people, it is the loss of a job, or another sign that lets you know this is the time. This is when trusting your gut will be the best compass to follow. If you experience an event that creates an overwhelming drive and determination to start your business, trust your instinct. Motivation may come from the fact that you are tired of living paycheck-to-paycheck or you see that your side business can really help someone in need while generating an income for you. The spark can come from a variety of different sources. "If opportunity doesn't knock, build a door." If you are waiting for a sign, maybe you have to get the ball rolling, and your own momentum will keep things moving forward. Waiting for the right time is a common trait in all of us, but sometimes you just have to take that leap of faith, no matter how small, to get you moving from a wantrepreneur to an entrepreneur.

How long will it take to become "successful?"

This is something that everyone itches to ask. "How long did it take before you became successful?" or "How long did it take to break even?" These are both legitimate questions that you need to take into consideration. Businesses can take years to break even, and when they do, their profit margins may be razor thin. This is a fact, especially with small businesses that start very small, with only your own savings. I thought that if only I bought A, B, and C, I would earn D. But in reality, I didn't know the true cost of running the business, as small as it was, while I was funding it myself. My simple bare bones mentality was only good for the first day, then expenses came up well beyond A, B, and C, all the way to Y, and then I earned Z. I didn't account for all the small expenses like printer ink, business checks, web hosting, fuel, and the larger expenses like insurance. All these things add up - especially printer ink.

The most expensive thing that will add up is your time. We all know that time is money. How will you be compensated for the time that you put into your start-up business? Notice that I said compensated, rather than paid. You will be your largest asset and your largest expense when you are sole proprietor. You are the most expensive person on the payroll, especially when you can't afford to pay yourself. If that isn't scary, you should get your head examined.

I learned from a fellow farmer that, no matter what, you pay your employees, your taxes, and your bills, and then the rest is yours. Well, in reality, it is all yours, and when expenses start to get high, you will feel it in your checkbook. You will want to cut back on the things I call "fluff" - all the tiny expenses that accumulate to take a huge chunk from your bottom line. The fact is that fiscal responsibility is wicked important, from one New Englander to the world.

This is where an accountant or bookkeeper comes into

play. They can be the ones to keep you on track, tell you what to spend your money on, and what to cut out. If you are using your income to buy things like promotional iPads for prospective clients, you may really need to reevaluate your finances. You should face the fact that you might not be able to get paid for a while after starting your business. You will get other compensation though. If you truly love what you are doing, providing a service or product to people, that is very rewarding. If you wake up and look forward to work each day, it is worth it.

You will have to define your own measure of success. It may be entirely financial for you. My definition of success has changed a few times. When I started out, I just wanted to sell all my plants. I would then strive to land another customer. I continued to set my sights higher so that the business would no longer need financial inputs from me, but would be sustainable on its own. At that point, the bank accounts were almost empty each spring before farmers' markets began again. I kept setting lofty goals, giving myself something higher for which to strive. I kept the vision in my mind every day, wrote it down, and had fun trying to reach that next level of success.

One of the biggest wins I've had so far in my journey happened recently. Getting into farmers' markets in my area is incredibly competitive and slightly political. As I said earlier, I applied to a whole list of markets, large and small, my first year. I had gotten into the Salem Farmers'

Market with pure luck, and then the Swampscott Farmers' Market, because they had just started and needed vendors. I had applied to this one other amazing market for three years in a row, always receiving a polite rejection. I had met the market manager at another market, and he was very nice to talk to. A year later, he returned to my stand, and we got to talking again. He was so impressed with my display and my produce that he encouraged me to apply again. Their market needed another vegetable grower because one would be leaving the following season. This market was always full, because vendors never leave. That is one great sign for someone that has vegetables to sell. He said that if I applied I would be accepted.

Reading this, you are probably saying, "Yippie, the kid was accepted to another market," but in my world, my business is part of me, and this was a huge game changer. My business had evolved greatly since the first farmers' market three years before. This was the farmer's equivalent to being asked to serve in the president's cabinet. It was one of those moments when I really felt like I and my business belonged. Not only did we belong, we were in demand. I like to think that I'm not your average vegetable grower. I am not conventional and I am not organic. I like to think that I am unconventional. I didn't just bring my vegetable in the worn-out field picking crates; I displayed the produce in wooden vegetable crates. The signs were clean, you knew who we were by our banner, and the staff all had matching shirts so you knew we worked there. I made vegetable buying an experience for customers. My system of setting up and selling wasn't built overnight. It is constantly evolving and changes with each market. I take pride in my stand, because I work hard to grow my crops. It would be a shame to sell them with any less pride.

The small wins in my experience, like being invited to an exclusive farmers' market, are the kinds of moments that reaffirm, "Hey, I must be doing something right." These are the kind of moments that make it worth all the fear and hard work. When I have a line of customers before the market even opens, and a separate line of people who just want to buy our eggs, I know it has been worth it. When I see a customer's shopping list and my last name is written next to certain items, I know I'm succeeding.

Your definition of success can be whatever you want. It could be as simple as setting aside one hour a day to think about and work on your business, and sticking to it. Your definition of successful could be making your first sale, and then making a bigger sale. I do know that your definition of success should be intangible. It can't just be a dollar amount, but something like the feeling of pride that comes from having satisfied customers, who not only buy your product, but they also recommend it to a friend.

Since your business is something you created out of your own thoughts, ideas, and dreams, you will be emotionally connected to it. Your business will be a big part of your life, because you own it. It is an emotional connection that I can't really explain. I don't want to tell you it is your baby, but in a way it is, because you created it. When your business is growing and doing well, you will move forward with it, you will be happy, and you will keep growing with it. When you experience a customer or competitor bad-mouthing you or your product or service, you will be offended. You will feel hurt. It will get you down, but don't let it keep you down. If someone doesn't like your product that is Ok. You can't please everyone.

"I don't know the key to success, but the key to failure is trying to please everybody."
— Bill Cosby

I love this quote, because it applies to more than just business. It applies to everything in life. If you spend all your time trying to make everyone else happy, you won't ever be happy yourself.

ORGANIZE AND PLAN

What if I'm not organized?

If you are not organized, here is one piece of advice: Learn to be. The only way to get better at organization is to try out different organizational techniques. There are volumes of books that address that very problem. Many people think that they aren't good at organization because they have never taken the time to see what works for them. My system wouldn't work for most. If you are thinking that I run all of my businesses electronically, you are wrong. I am an old school, hard-copy person. I still believe in paper (remember my printer ink bill?). If you think that my desk is neat and tidy, it is not. In fact, innocent bystanders in my office would think that a file cabinet puked onto a dining room table. I have piles and lists. This system works for me, because I need to physically see things, even if I have to kill some trees in the process.

I am an avid list maker. I make lists on scrap paper, sides of produce boxes, and legal pads. This book was effectively written on all of those media. I write lists about farming, books, personal tasks, and ideas. I will think of something, and if I don't write it down immediately, I will forget about it and it will be lost forever.

I know some people, who can operate their entire business from their iPad, never having to shuffle through a file box. I might not trust technology as readily as some, but I know how my mind works, and that if I don't write things down, they will never get done.

Finding your own organizational system that helps you keep everything in order, show up on time, and pay your bills will be a challenge. At times you will wonder how anyone ever got a business off the ground with all the bills, mail, payroll, taxes, invoices, checks, and everything else getting thrown at you. It will be difficult, but once you find the system that works for you when your business is in its infancy, you will just have to magnify it as you grow to keep up with the scope of your business. This is when a bookkeeper and a payroll company can come in handy.

These people can keep you on track with your finances, make sure you are reporting earnings correctly, and help you play by all the rules that the IRS has. This will be a huge weight lifted off your shoulders, allowing you to focus on the 100 other things that will come your way. Because you are the owner, sole proprietor, and master of your business universe, you will know everything that goes on in your business from day one. All the information, numbers, figures, and important dates will be in your head, but that only helps you. What if someone besides you needed that information? Organization will be critically important if you get audited or experience circumstances that keep you away from work. Even if this doesn't happen to you, organize it for your sake. Free up some of the space in your brain for new thoughts and new ideas so that you can stay creative and at the cutting edge.

If you become buried in paperwork and "things" to deal with, this is the perfect time to ask for help. Look for a friend, who is very organized, and ask for help. This will circle back to the fact that there are people who want to see you succeed. Without paying someone to organize your life, like the people on the show *Hoarders*, a friend can help pull you out of your own quagmire of business and put you on track to be more organized. You may not be able to pay this person, but you could take them to dinner, or offer them services or products in return. Just because you aren't organized doesn't mean that you can't be. You will have to take the time to figure out the system that works best for you to keep track of everything that goes into running your business. I will be honest, sometimes running your business really gets in the way of running your business. There are days that I have to practically chain myself to my desk to get things done when it is perfect weather to go out and work in the fields. Running the business sometimes gets in the way of the fun part of my job, which is farming.

CHRISTOPHER GRANT

LEARN TO JUGGLE

Running your own business involves handling many different day-to-day tasks, which can be difficult to keep up in the air at once. Juggling them all is a feat in itself. Along with the business, young entrepreneurs have to balance school, family, church, other jobs and obligations, and maybe even a social life at the end of it all. This challenge falls under a topic on which there are many books: time management. Managing your valuable time to make sure that all of your tasks get done is the only way to…well, get things done. However you manage your many obligations as an entrepreneur, you are bound to get tunnel vision. You will get so caught up with "urgent" demands that each molehill task will look like a mountain. You will get stressed and you may even make yourself sick.

At this point, take a look at your business from 30,000 feet, as if you were looking out from the window of an airplane. You will soon realize that in the big scheme of things your small business really is small, and that there is far more to life than the tasks at hand. The mountains you were dreading are only grains of sand now, and you can return to them the next day, if possible, with a clear mind. When the time comes that you have employees whom you can trust, delegate tasks to them and let them make the job their own. This will take the stress off of you and give the employee a sense of meaning and inclusiveness that will breed success. Some days, the best thing you can do is take the rest of the day off. Go ahead and get out of the picture for some time off. With all the hard work you put in, you will deserve some time off. It will be the best thing for you.

Dropping a Ball…

From time to time, you will drop one of those balls that you are frantically tossing up in the air. We will call this failing. So what? You failed. Whether your mistake is big or small, as an entrepreneur it will probably cost you money. When a mistake costs you money, you most likely won't make the same mistake again. Take the time to learn from your mistakes and failures. If you don't see a failure as an opportunity to learn, it will always be a failure. Take responsibility for the mistake, own up to it, and move on. There is a little tough love for you.

I GOOGLED "BUSINESS PLANS" AND ALMOST PUKED!

I did too. I thought it would be a good idea to get some advice about business plans, but with all the crap Google threw my way, I had no idea whom to trust. If you Google "sample business plans," you will find examples of business plans for every kind of business in every industry you can think of. Some plans are elaborate pdfs that are completely prepared and cover every aspect of an imaginary company. Others are excerpts from real business plans. You will come across a spectrum of plans from long documents with a lot of "fluffy" information to the plans that are "cut and dry" and to the point. Looking over a few plans will be the best way to learn what you really need to include in your plan. They will provide rough guidelines for what a basic business plan needs.

Your first real business plan will be a huge undertaking. You'll not only be telling people all about your company inside and out, but you'll also have to make big-picture statements about the direction and mission of your business. The first mission statement I wrote was this simple: *Grow good food.* My first business plan was a product of a college class. I chose to work alone, because I actually had a business. Other students took ideas out of the sky and had to work hard to generate a fake plan that would, let's face it, may never actually come to life (that is me being a pessimist). I had put off building a business plan, mainly because I thought, "Who would read it?"

When I finally had to write one and get graded on it, I knew I had a deadline. I wrote and wrote and wrote, all about the background information, plans, goals, and ambitions of my business. I poured it all out on the table for the teacher to see. I got a great grade on the business plan, but I also ended up with a living document that laid out my entire business. Anyone could look at it and learn everything about me and my creation. Most companies that write and stick to business plans go back to them periodically to reevaluate, because it is a "living document" that is always changing.

I hope that you and your business will grow. As you expand and grow your product line, the services you offer, and the company's infrastructure, now is the time that a real business plan should be drafted. If you make the commitment to write a full business plan for your own use, or to use for investors or submit to a bank, be honest with your goals and expectations. If you are not a good writer, ask for help. If you cannot decide how to word the sentences or what belongs and doesn't belong in the plan, ask for help. There are professional business plan writers who will take your "golden idea" and turn it into a fully-developed business plan ready for the loan officer. But at the beginning, you can get an enormous start by pecking away on your own at the huge task of writing a business plan. Again, a plan is only good if you have the discipline to stick to it day-to-day.

"A goal is a dream with a deadline."
– Napoleon Hill

I continue to tell you to start. That is true, the most important step is starting, but don't forget to keep moving. The goals that you set for your new business have to be SMART. This is for all of my friends, who are a product of the FFA. SMART stands for: Specific, Measureable, Attainable, Realistic or Relevant, and Time-bound. Any business or marketing teacher will drill this into your head as well as the curriculum for the FFA, formerly known as the Future Farmers of America. It is a simple idea that if every one of your goals you set follows the criteria of SMART goals, you can achieve them.

When you set a goal write down all of your thoughts about your golden idea or dream business one night a week for a month. These should be very specific, measureable, attainable, realistic, and time bound. Very SMART, if I say so myself. When you begin setting goals like: buy a giant warehouse and hire an assistant on the first day you decide to start a business, that is not very SMART and your day will start and end in stress and disappointment. If I do not set deadlines for my projects, they simply won't get done.

I have colleagues that believe they do their best work at the last minute. I don't believe in that philosophy, because I do not do very good work when I am stressed. When I plan to order seeds, I have a very specific list, with the amount of seeds I need, not too many varieties that I will never plant, and it is ordered by a specific date. If I didn't set up my deadline, I would be ordering whatever I wanted at the last minute. For writing this book, I set a deadline to have it done by my birthday, but that is in June, when farmers are busy. This goal was not realistic for my schedule. I didn't throw it all away, I just made another goal to have it done by the first of the year, nailed it!

If you set out to solve all the world's problems on day one, your to do list will be so overwhelming that you may never want to get out of bed. The "to do" list of new business owners is never ending, but it is not impossible. Remember, so many people have been just where you are today, and have made it work. Every company started out as a dream or idea. They put that dream into motion, no matter what stood in their way. Even without the internet and Google, businesses were started, now that makes it all look easy huh?

"The secret of getting ahead is getting started. The secret of getting started is breaking your complex overwhelming tasks into manageable tasks, and then starting on the first one."
— Mark Twain

Not every plan works out.

I used my family's land as the hub of my business. To take the farm to the next level, I devised a plan to present to my family. There is a fund for graduates of UMass agricultural programs, which allows them to borrow money for their agricultural business. I wrote out an elaborate plan that I used to apply for funding from this agricultural fund. It outlined my need to buy new equipment, supplies, and marketing services for Grant Family Farm, along with hiring another person. I had it in my mind that this was the only way to get to the next level. I had my plan in hand and sprung it on my parents, aunt, and uncle one night. I was so nervous, waiting to hear their reaction. They read the plan and to my surprise they simultaneously jumped for joy to the accompaniment of an 80s music montage.

Okay, that did not happen. That night was actually one of the worst nights of my life. Although they were nice about it, they didn't want to use the land as security for the loan. Each idea I had presented was shot down. I was sick to my stomach, ran out to my car, and had a panic attack. My own family was frightened by my reaction. They believed in me and supported me, but I was asking too much. I started the year off with that wound still healing. Today, I still think about my heart being in my throat as they listed off why they wouldn't help or allow this to happen on the farm. I could have closed up everything and walked away, but I didn't. This was just a setback. Sure it sucked at the time, but looking back, it was probably for the best. If I was going to give up, I would have given up long before then.

"Courage doesn't always roar. Sometimes courage is the quiet voice at the end of the day saying, "I will try again tomorrow."
— Mary Anne Radmacher

When you present your plan or ideas to people, don't be shy. Be confident with your plan, but not cocky, because you had the guts to make it. Don't shy away because someone else doesn't like your idea. Who are they to judge your plans, ideas, or dreams, when you are the one actually going after them? I am a doer. I get things done. The day that I stop thinking like that and start believing that someone else will do them for me, is the day I shut it all down. I've decided that while everyone else is watching "Survivor" on TV, I'm going to get out there and **be** one in real life (take that world).

GAME CHANGERS

Some of you may want to create social change and dub yourself a social entrepreneur. Social entrepreneurs are people, who start businesses that are change based and geared towards changing something in the world. Goals of social entrepreneurs are all over the map literally. The goal could deal with hunger, human rights, developing nations, fair trade, or anything that you are truly passionate about. Social entrepreneurs are those that thrive on the fact that they are contributing to solving a problem in the world and making a difference. The business can be either a non-profit or a for profit. I cannot say too much about forming a non-profit business other than the fact that the structure of the business is complex. If you are planning on starting a non-profit you should seek council in the organization of such a business.

I was once asked how people, who form or work at non-profit organizations, get paid. You cannot forget that non-profit organizations do make money, and part of the expense of many organizations is salaries for employees, who make the organization work. If you have your heart set on developing a non-profit business without much knowledge in the specific area of non-profits, I would recommend finding a like minded organization and work with them. This could be paid or on a volunteer basis, the knowledge you gain would be priceless.

I once thought of starting a non-profit farming group for people with developmental disabilities, instead of creating another entity, I got involved with an agency that places clients with disabilities in jobs like farming. This has been a match made in heaven. When their van shows up, my day is made. I have so much passion and respect for people with disabilities, and love that I can have them work on my farm. In return they earn money on an hourly basis that they can spend how they wish, giving them so much pride. That is one way I can use my business to make the world a little better, even if it just a hand full of people a few times a week, without starting a non-profit of my own.

> *"There's lots of bad reasons to start a company. But there's only one good, legitimate reason, and I think you know what it is: it's to change the world."* — Phil Libin

Right now it is sexy to be a social entrepreneur, mainly because there are so many things that need fixing in this world. If you are passionate about something, and you are so driven to start a business in hopes of making change, I applaud you and your determination. Entrepreneurship is a labor of love, whereas social entrepreneurship takes so much more determination. Why? Because you are out to change the world, and change is slow and the world is a big place.

> *"Vision without action is merely a dream. Action without vision just passes the time. Vision with action can change the world"*
> — Joel A. Barker

CHRISTOPHER GRANT

WHERE DO I BELONG?

As you and your business grow, you may have to decide if you want to specialize or diversify. One option is to specialize in one narrowly-defined market, keeping your product or service tailored to their specific needs. You would only focus on offering your specialized product or service to that market and doing it well. One example of this is a pool supply business. The company is committed to selling only goods or services related to pools and pool supplies. The business may have a large selection of products, but they are specialists in pool supplies. On the other hand, you may want expand your business by diversifying your product or service.

This may be the most common form of growth or expansion for young entrepreneurs. This business model would open your one business to offer a wide variety of products or services in a wide range of industries. Many large companies diversify to offer what competitors offer. This is why you can now find Wal-Marts all over the world offering inexpensive products. That was the founding goal of Wal-Mart - affordable goods. They are large stores that offer a wide selection of goods. Now, with the establishment of Super Wal-Marts, they offer food, groceries, pharmacy services, vision care, auto repair, photo processing…the growth is mind blowing. They diversified to the point that they really are the one-stop shopping destination for a very large portion of the world's population. They have cornered the market by not just opening up all these different facets of business within one store, but by doing it cheaper than anyone else out there. Whether or not you agree with Wal-Mart and their way of doing business, they are one of the best examples of really diversifying. Wal-Mart also offers pools and pool supplies.

Whether you choose to remain as a pool supply business to the specialized market you started out serving, or diversify into complementary products or services, you should do so slowly, and only after thorough market research. Filling a niche or finding your "thing" is the place to start.

A farmers' market is an incubator for many businesses besides farms. There are crafters, bakers, soap makers, wineries, and other foods you wouldn't likely find at your grocery store. When a new vendor shows up, I always make a point to introduce myself, and when they aren't busy, ask how they got started. They usually respond with their personal story, which–after I heard a couple–all started to sound alike: "I saw a need for _____, and I knew I could fill it." This is the case with the stand that carries guacamole at the market, the woman who makes goat's milk soap, the group that sells authentic Greek foods, and the new vendor, who just started making dairy-free ice cream.

They all saw the demand, and they knew that they could fill it, or make it better than the company that is already making the product. The guacamole people have an amazing product without the preservatives you would find in prepared guacamole from a grocery store. They knew they could do it better. The woman who hand crafts goat's milk soap was tired of the harsh chemicals in regular soap so she started to make her own and it flourished into a business. The booth that carries authentic Greek foods was dreamt up by a girl, who just returned from living in Greece and wanted to get authentic Mediterranean fare to the public with her family's recipes. The business that sells lactose-free ice cream started after the owner had to stop eating dairy products, and found that the ice cream available to the masses was expensive and not that great.

These simple businesses each started with one thing that they wanted to change. One thing that they knew they could do better than anyone else out there. They saw a need and they filled it. They could have sat around waiting for better soap brands to come out or ice cream manufactures to catch up with the demand and make a better product, but they didn't. They took it into their own hands to make something better not just for themselves, but for their customers and anyone else who benefits from their products.

When you find your "thing," or the strongest attribute that makes you and your business outstanding, stick with it. I say this because some people overlook the opportunity to fill a niche because they can't recognize what is so special about them.

As a small business, you won't be able to offer your customers everything under the sun, so you have to focus on the things that make you unique. For me it is the small family farm that produces products that other people don't grow. I grow unique vegetables, free-range eggs, and affordable flowers. I grow vegetables like kale, bok choy, kohlrabi, and salad turnips, while everyone else is selling cucumbers, tomatoes, and corn. I sell eggs from chickens that I raise free range, while other vendors buy their eggs to re-sell. I grow flowers that are affordable because everyone loves flowers, but they are usually expensive. These descriptions of my niche show what makes my business stand out and what has made it successful.

If you are running a used bookstore, and you are only focused on building your inventory to fill the space in your shop, you may miss the reason why people come to your bookstore instead of the next one. The customers may come to your shop to not only buy the books, but also to sit and read in the comfortable space. If you go ahead filling that space with products, you are missing your niche of having a welcoming area for your customers to enjoy.

Identify what it is that makes you stand out from your competition and stick to it. This isn't meant to make you put all of your eggs in one basket (pardon the pun from the egg farmer). It is a special balance of doing what you do well even better, and experimenting in the diversifying of the business as described above. Find what you do well, and keep building on it. If you are going to do something, you might as well do it right.

In the hustle and bustle of entrepreneurship, you may be enticed to copy someone else's business. If you admire something that another business does well, you don't need to copy it to be like them. Take one aspect of the business and use it as a template for your own. I admire many farms for their involvement in their community; I won't copy their programs, but will find ways to get more involved with my own community. It is kind of like when you were in school and had to write a research paper. You could not use someone else's words, but you could put their ideas into your own words, making it your own. My teachers used to say, "Plagiarism is against the law! You will go to jail!" I don't want to go to jail.

CHRISTOPHER GRANT

HOW DO I DO IT?

Whatever you do with your business, make sure you do it consistently. That sounds like a given in the planning stages, but when the rubber meets the road, it is crucial. My bookkeeper gives me this lecture all the time, and I think I'm finally getting it.

Think about the businesses you use every day. Why do you patronize them? Businesses that offer the same experience every day to their customers are the ones that people return to. We are comfort-seeking creatures, who like consistency. We like knowing what to expect and being able to find a comfort zone.

I am definitely a creature of habit. I go to the Agawam Diner in Rowley, Massachusetts for three to four meals per week. The restaurant is a typical diner car, the waitresses are all friendly and know my name. If you are looking to order a strong drink, you are out of luck. Coffee, water, or Coke is all they pour. If you are looking for a glass of wine and chef-inspired dishes, you are out of luck. The coffee is good, but not great. Cash only, and you have to pay Andy on the way out, unless you get there before him. Sit where you like, and yes, the seats at the counter squeak. The rolls are always the same and come with the meal if you ask for them - make sure you do. For breakfast I get one pancake or hash and eggs over easy, both with white toast and bacon. For lunch I get the cheeseburger special, no fries, rolls, and a Coke. For dinner I get the fried clam strip roll or hot turkey sandwich with gravy on the side. If they changed beef I would know. If they changed gravy, I would know. I go there because I know it will always be the same. It is great food, a good value, and good people, consistently.

This principle applies to all types of business. If you are going to be the cheap provider, be the cheap provider consistently. If you are going to be the high-end provider, be the high-end provider consistently. The same thing goes for the middle-of-the-road providers.

The perfect example of a business that thrives on terrible service is the Dick's Last Resort restaurant chain. In most major cities in America, there is a Dick's franchise. People flock to these establishments because their servers are, well… dicks. They are trained to be mean, swear, and make off-color remarks to customers. Customers go just for the upside-down experience of being treated poorly. The food is okay, and they give you a free beer glass on your way out, but from the time you enter you are treated like crap. Some patrons are even given a handmade paper hat shaped like a certain organ that says something lewd on it. Why do people go there? Because they know what to expect! Every time they go there they expect mediocre food and drinks, and a waitress who will scream, "What the hell do you want to drink?" if you are not paying attention when she is taking your order. If you are into that, give it a try.

I like using restaurants as examples of business concepts, because we all go to them, and we are all critical. There are ones we go to often, and ones we try once or twice and then never go to again. Some restaurants are better than others. A restaurant opened on a road I drive multiple times a week. The food was said to be "okay" but the bar was the main attraction. The owners began adding on attractions to generate buzz about the business. They went out and bought plastic palm trees and rope lights to brighten up the place. Signs started coming out along the road saying, "kids eat free," then "35 cent wing night," then "Sushi Wednesday 5-10 pm & Friday 4-10 pm." Really? Sushi by appointment only?

The menu was growing, to the point where everyone in the building could be eating a different dish at one time. The nightly menu that included "Mexican night" and other gimmicks was just too much in such a competitive dining town. This new restaurant is so complex that passersby are put off by the change of menu every night. If you were to tell me we were going there on Tuesday, I wouldn't know what to expect on the menu. With my luck there would also be a live band, and I do not like a drum kit next to my table. The business is seriously lacking consistency. As a geek, who picks up on that stuff,

I can't tell you how long they will continue to operate. I hope they find their niche and stick to it soon, so we know when to get Asian food and when to get Mexican food.

Whatever you do, do it consistently. When you start to veer off your plan on a whim, not only will your customers know, but your staff, and anyone else involved will be lost. Change takes time. I think we all know how Rome was built, right? Not in a day, and look how well that worked out. Your business should be a product of evolution, growing, and changing slowly. When I was 16, I am sure my business looked like it was being run by a 16-year-old, no matter how hard I tried to make it look legit. When you get excited or nervous and start making sharp turns to get places, you will only confuse people, hinder them from knowing what to expect, and turn them off. If you ever see me rolling sushi one week and grooming dogs the next week at my farmers' markets, remind me of this important lesson to be consistent.

YOU WILL WORK

I know that I have been telling you all about fears and how to overcome them when thinking about starting a business. I would be a bad friend if I didn't tell you just how hard the task of starting a business is in reality. If you are thinking that everything will be just sunshine and lollipops, it's not. With all of the things that can go right in your business career, there are also many things that can go wrong. To call entrepreneurship a roller coaster ride would be an understatement. There are highs and lows, ups and downs, and twists and turns that may take you off course and get you down. If you have the true spirit of an entrepreneur, you will be able to roll with the punches.

Entrepreneurship is a messy occupation...

When things don't go as planned, you will be able to pick up the pieces where they fall and put them back together. You will be pulled in many directions both mentally and physically. There will be times when your mind will be buried in your business, thinking about what's next and all the things that you have to do to keep moving forward. You will have to sacrifice things that you want to do for the things that you need to do. When money is tight, difficult decisions have to be made. When you don't know the right answers your dream job can, at times, be a nightmare. You may find that the business you have dreamed about for years has taken over your world and is practically sucking the life out of you. The stress of navigating your business through the unknown is sickening.

Now, you may think that I am trying to scare you out of taking the leap toward starting your business, but I'm not. I am just letting you know that when things look bad, you get bogged down, and you feel like there is no way out, remember that you are the creator of your business. If there is anyone in the world that can stop, take a step back, and reassess the situation, it's you. My goal is not to scare you, but to convince you to start small. When you picture a business being small and simple, you will soon find that the scary parts are in the small details that arise in the process.

> *"It's the little details that are vital. Little things make big things happen."*— John Wooden

Taking the step to start your own business will be one of the most liberating things you will do in your life. It will also be the most challenging. If you are willing to work, fight, learn, and adjust around the rest of life, you will be successful. If you are the kind of person who will make time in your life to seriously follow your dream and fight to make it all work, go for it. If you want to start a business because it will be an easy way to make money, you are in for a rude awakening.

Entrepreneurship offers a great lifestyle. I've never been the cubicle type. I'm not even the indoor type! My office is at the top of a tractor in the morning, and in the dirt pulling beets in the afternoon. My business is seasonal, but it's full-time year-round. I have four months to make enough money for the year. I have the flexibility to go to the diner for breakfast with the old folks, but I also don't get sick pay for when I can't get any work done. I can take the day off to go hiking, but I don't get paid vacation time. While most people work from 9 am to 5 pm, I work from 5 am to 9 pm. I can't take weekends off in the summer, because if I don't go to the farmers' market, I don't make money.

On Thursday nights, when my friends are at the bars, I am getting home from being on my feet for four hours at a farmers' market and only want to go to bed. People must think I am crazy to work so much and fight so hard to keep myself afloat in this economy in the business of agriculture. To sum it all up, I'm not living a "normal" life, and I'm fine with that. To be a successful entrepreneur, you can't settle for normal or ordinary. To be successful, you have to be so crazy that you will work even if you don't get paid.

"Entrepreneurship is living a few years of your life like most people won't so you can spend the rest of your life like most people can't."
— Unknown

Passion for your industry is something that you will need to have in order to be successful. When I start talking about my farm, I can go on for days, because I love it. Greenhouses and farming are my passion. When I walk into a production greenhouse, whatever season it is, I love looking down the center aisle at the tags and pots all aligned like soldiers waiting to be called into action. Smaller hoop houses are my favorite because growers, who use them, have such a connection to their crop.

Whether growing plants in a million-dollar greenhouse range or a second-hand hoop house with pallets on the ground, farmers generally all do it for the same reason. I love setting the plows in the ground for the first time each spring to turn field of green over to reveal the soil underneath. The ability to sow seeds and watch them germinate, grow, and produce fruit to harvest. When a new batch of fluffy chicks arrive in the spring. I love the ability to watch the seasons unfold in front of my eyes and under my feet. There is a lasting joy in knowing you have helped create something out of the earth and have used it to provide for one of humankind's most basic needs.

This all sounds picturesque doesn't it? It might even sound like it's too good to be true. I joke that I have a passion for poultry, but I really do. I love agriculture, and I am crazy enough to own a farm in the state with the highest agricultural land value in the country. At a time when businesses are going under, I am fighting to keep mine afloat. Could I go off and work at someone else's farm? Technically, yes. But I chose the road less traveled, and, not to sound too sappy, it really has made all the difference.

During my senior year of college I was selected for the perfect internship. When I say perfect, I mean it. This was the dream internship for any college student. I was selected to be a social media intern at a catalog company that sells farm supplies. This was a match made in heaven. Not only do I love farming and get the catalog delivered to my door and read it cover to cover, but I am also a social media addict. As are most college students. I was hired to work with the marketing department to design and implement social media content for fifteen to twenty hours a week. I got to sit on Facebook, Twitter, and YouTube for hours at a time, only now I got paid to do it!

What college student, or any twenty something for that matter, wouldn't like to do that? They set me up with a cubicle, computer, phone, social media accounts, I had it all (even a stuffed giraffe). Since you haven't met me, I'll tell you that I am six-feet two-inches tall, my legs being five feet of that. Fitting into this cubicle was difficult. I had to wear business clothing, except on this thing called casual Friday, something I was new to. As it turned out, I was a social media machine, writing content about products that I knew and used. These content pieces went to editors and then came back to me to schedule them for release, on whatever site they belonged.

I am sad to say that the "wooh factor" wore off quickly for me. I was having a hard time staying inside ALL DAY. I was the weirdo taking a break to walk around the building in January and eating lunch outside in February. I was pretty close to taking up smoking just so I could have another reason to stand outside. I enjoyed the social media, the company, and the people I worked with, some I still have connection with through, you guessed it, social media.

After about two months, I had to leave. I gave my two week notice, and left. When I found the internship online, I had this hope in the back of my mind that maybe this could be my next big thing that I do. In reality, social media is still in its infancy, so there is so much that is evolving and changing every day. For me that was exciting. But I quickly learned that the office life wasn't for me. The experience made me realize that even though I thought I knew what I wanted, I just didn't belong. I didn't belong inside, wearing a collared shirt, khaki pants, and eating lunch within a certain number of minutes.

Sometimes, when I'm pulling carrots when its 100 degrees or moving squash when its below freezing or when I am knee deep in mud after getting a tractor stuck, I think...maybe I could have made it work. But when I am getting hugs from customers at a farmers' market or eating supper that came entirely from my fields, I know that I am right where I need to be.

> *"One of the huge mistakes people make is that they try to force an interest on themselves. You don't choose your passions; your passions choose you."*— *Jeff Bezos*

(Just the founder and CEO of a little-known online store called Amazon.)

My drive comes from a former boss and good friend. Working late in the greenhouse potting up Easter lily bulbs, we were talking about how we work later than everyone else and how it feels like she never leaves the place. She even would make deals with me that if I stayed for another hour, she would write down that I stayed for two. When I was 16 and in need of gas money, I would always stay with her. One evening, she said, "I don't know who said it before, but if you love what you do, you won't ever work a day in your life." This saying follows me everywhere I go and I will never forget it.

That is a lot of passion, huh? And that's why I do a job that most people don't really think about. So many people think food comes from the grocery store, not a farm. But I am proud to say, I have never worked a day in my life.

WHAT IF?

I am asked questions frequently when I start talking business ideas with both young and old people. One of the best is "What if I get audited by the IRS?" That one is easy. If you have your records in order, a bookkeeper or accountant to back you up, and you didn't do anything stupid, don't worry. When it comes to financial fears, believe me, I too fear the IRS, but I am honest with my bookkeeper, and I trust her.

The *what if* question is endless. What if I do XYZ? What if I don't? And so on and so forth. What if customers ask to work with me but I'm not set up yet? What if the customer base I counted on, as being an easy sell, isn't receptive to my new product? All these variables that fall under the category of unknown are scary. Even for me today, the *what if* is scary.

If you get caught up in the *what if*s, you are going to be questioning way more than just your dream business. The *what if* happens to everyone in many different situations. What if I had asked her out before she met him? What if my car had not broken down before my interview? What if I wasn't born? Okay, that one is kind of creepy to think about, but you get the idea. We are all victims of our minds wandering to the place of *what if*, and then worrying about all the things that could potentially go wrong, even before something like a business exists.

Once when I was going through a hard time, I was talking to a friend on the phone. I went on a rant of consecutive *what if* scenarios that could occur in my life and all the horrible things that would then happen. She stopped me and said, "But Chris, what if none of that stuff happened? Where would you be?" I stopped. I didn't have anything to say. She continued and asked, "What if everything you are worried about never happens, or, better yet, happens in the complete opposite way?" Now that is something for you to think about. When you are faced with so many *what if* questions and unknowns, especially in business, it is scary, but most of them will never occur.

One thing that I often forget when thinking about an unknown or a *what if* is that people have started businesses before. If you think about it, although not everyone in the world will take the leap from being a wantrepreneur to an entrepreneur, there have been many people who have done it before you. Entrepreneurs tackle these fears every day to keep moving forward toward achieving their dreams. If you look at all your unknowns and *what if*s from 30,000 feet, they will seem miniscule compared to the other problems in the world.

Your mind is a dangerous place to go all by yourself.

Finding a mentor in your industry or related field, who has been where you, too, want to go is another great way to overcome your fears. I hope they don't just pick you up, put you and your business on their shoulder, and leap over the scary parts for you, because that won't help. Like a fitness trainer, they can guide and inform, but can't do the heavy lifting for you. Your strength will come from the tough times that you got through with your own hard work. Every business is different, so the journey will be different for everyone. A mentor will allow you to have one more voice of reason to guide you through the tough times. They can give you advice based on their own fears and how they overcome them.

There are always going to be aspects of running your business that you don't enjoy. For example, I hate talking on the phone and about myself. An employer once asked me why I hated calling people on the phone. I told him I always felt like I was bothering them, or catching them at a bad time. He laughed and said, "Why do you think they have phones? They have them so you can bother them and do business with them." People are busy, but if they are too busy to be nice on the phone, they don't deserve your business. People might answer the phone with a programmed response ready, but if you are prepared to tell them who you are, what you want, and you are polite about it, they will usually be polite in return. The truth is, I don't always know who is going to answer a call, or if their cat got hit by a slow-moving parade that morning. I don't know if I have the right extension, if the person is at lunch, or if they can even help me. And I won't know if I don't call.

Maybe they are the right person and just won $100 on a scratch lottery ticket that morning. The fact is that I will only find out if I pick up the phone and call. I used to practice what I would say. Now, I just think ahead for a few seconds, and then go for it. I am happy on the phone, even if I have personal crap going on. For all I know, the person on the other line is just as scared to call me as I am of them. You never know all the factors going on so just go ahead and call.

"A ship is safe in harbor is safe, but that's not what ships are built for" – William G.T. Shedd

NOT ENOUGH?

Whenever I get to talking to people about business, their dreams, and anything else that is coming up in the conversation of the moment, I will always ask, "Why haven't you started? Why haven't you gone for it?" More times than I would like, I hear that the reason someone didn't go for it was because they thought they were under-qualified to be an entrepreneur. This is one of the greatest fears of any wantrepreneur - the idea in their mind that they were never good in school, that they didn't finish college. But you don't need to have a degree in what you want your business to be, and you don't need to have experience running any kind of business. Experience will come with as you create and run your business.

"Remember, amateurs built the ark, professionals built the Titanic." – Unknown

The excuses that make you believe you are inadequate will hold you back forever if you let them. This notion won't only hold you back from starting your dream business, but from achieving anything at all. If you don't think you are qualified to start a business, enjoy this example.

When you are in second grade, you want to be just like everyone else - wear the same shirt with your favorite cartoon character on it, buy lunch instead of bring it, and have a cool show-and-tell item. But I was different. In second grade, there was something I couldn't do that everyone else could do. In kindergarten, a few kids could do it. In first grade, even more kids could do it, and by second grade, almost everyone could do this but me. I couldn't read. It's not that I didn't try to read.

Believe me, my parents and teachers all tried to get me to read, but nothing ever stuck. Not only could I not read, but I was also the best at not reading. I avoided it at all costs. I would go to the bathroom before it would be my turn to read aloud, until one day the law caught up to me. I was called on to read. I looked down at the page, looked at the first word and…I didn't know it. There were a few words I had memorized, could recognize, could sound out or figure out, but this wasn't one of them. I didn't know what to say.

To my surprise, because of this event, I got to miss an entire day of school, ride the train, go to the museum of science, and then eventually go to the doctor. This doctor tested me on how I sounded things out, what I could read, what I couldn't read, and what I would do when I was stuck.

Two weeks later, a letter came in the mail that said I was dyslexic. When my parents told me, I didn't care. I was a little kid, what was I going to do? Ask for a second opinion? I was put into the Wilson reading program to catch me up with the rest of the class. Three days a week, I would have to go to school an hour early to go learn how to read, starting with my ABCs. I hated it, and was miserable through the entire process. My parents would drop me off, and sometimes I would just go out back to the playground and wait for the busses to show up. Despite all the fighting with my parents and teachers, after over a year in the program I could finally read.

I wasn't at the same level as other kids my age, but I could read. I'm sure you're thinking, *Thank God. Now that this kid can read, his life must be all unicorns and candy rain and he can tell me how to start my business.* But there is more. With all of the time and energy going into getting me to be able to read, everything else fell by the wayside. I kept falling further behind the rest of the class, not only because I was diagnosed with a learning disability, but because I hated school. I didn't like my classes, teachers, or many of the kids, because everything came easily to them. For me, learning is tough. I was swept through middle school because I had this stamp on my forehead that said dyslexic. They pulled me through to graduate to eighth grade.

When I started high school, my world was changed. I walked into one of the classrooms and saw written on the chalkboard, "Here we learn by doing." I didn't go to a typical high school. I went to Essex Agricultural and

Technical High School. We learned about plant science, animal science, and environmental science on top of all the usual academic content. For the first time in my life, I was learning how I learn.

I can't read a book and know how to do anything. But if I actually look at a picture or get my hands, God forbid, dirty, I learn easily. I had spent years sitting in rows of desks being taught at, and never really learning. And yet here, when I was outside, building walls, fixing engines, halter breaking calves, and testing water, I thrived. I didn't graduate at the top of my class, because I still had a hard time in academic classes, but I was able to use my learning style in those classes too. I don't have a learning disability; I think the education system has a teaching disability.

The idea that stuffing kids in a classroom and teaching them to fill in the right bubbles to pass a test is not education. Education happens when a girl, who lives in an apartment building, overcomes her fear of animals to the point that she volunteers to help halter break calves after school. Education is when a kid decides to get a job as a landscaper for the summer, because he loves it, rather than playing video games. School should be a process to help find your passion, not a series of facts to be memorized. Yes, there are things all children need to learn but there can be a balance between the book learning and the hands-on learning.

But I digress. I started my business in high school because I had the drive and the skills that only high school plant geeks like myself have. As a kid, who wasn't expected to do well in high school, I even went to college and got an associate's degree in fruit and vegetable crops from the Stockbridge School of Agriculture. I received my bachelor of science in plant, soil, and insect science with a concentration in business from the University of Massachusetts at Amherst, all while operating my business.

I wasn't valedictorian, I didn't go to an Ivy League college, and I never managed a business in my life. My passion has driven me to learn on the job. The idea that only "smart" people start businesses is not true. Those, who thrive in school, are often the people who end up working for established businesses and who would never actually start a business. They are valuable to someone, and will take a job doing what their diploma says they can do. That is fine, and the world wouldn't operate without them. Going back to having a rewarding career. The people, who start their own businesses, on the other hand, are the ones who are daring, the ones who are creative and can think outside the box. I am talking about the round pegs in the square holes again, the crazy ones. That might just be you.

If you think you need an MBA to be an entrepreneur, you may be thinking way too much. Think of two famous examples - Bill Gates and Mark Zuckerberg. They were both on track to graduate from great colleges, but each of them quit to follow their dream, and look at them now. Those are two crazy examples, and you shouldn't try and be like them, mainly because they are certainly very unique examples. Still, there are countless other examples of successful entrepreneurs, who built great businesses and made themselves great with what they had. So you should look around for other entrepreneurs in your industry or in your area. You may just find that they aren't all "geniuses." They may be quirky, weird, even normal, and possibly they are the kind of person that is outside your wildest expectations of what an entrepreneur should be. By doing this, you just may find that you have a lot more to offer than you think. Don't sell yourself short.

> *"Formal education will make you a living; self-education will make you a fortune."*
> — Jim Rohn

When I first entered college, people were always asking one another, "So, what's your major?" There were sexy majors like political science, biology, gender studies, and, of course, business. Whatever you choose to do down the road, as an entrepreneur you are going to have to learn about business. I never went to college for business specifically, but like most universities, mine required a few courses that were not directly tied to my major.

I strongly recommend taking a few business courses, if you are at the point in your education when you can do so. You will probably sit in a huge lecture hall with both business majors and anyone else who desires the knowledge. The first day of class is always the most motivating. No matter which business course you take, the professor will likely slap a statistic on the board that gives you the impression that every business will fail and you will never be able to make it "out there," wherever "out there" is.

In the meantime, until you have the opportunity to fail in the world of business, they will fill your brain with everything you want to know about franchising and shareholders and taxes. The instructor, of the class, may have spent decades working toward a Ph.D. in business, but they will cover the topic in a blink of an eye, or 14 weeks. They may have some "real world" experience in business or management, but they may not bring it to the table. The experience can be very circumstantial. The instructor will give you all of the book information about starting your business, seeking investors, and mass merchandising, always coming back to the likelihood of "failure," as tough love. I put that word in quotation marks because I will address it later.

After taking a general business course, find out if your institution offers classes that are more specific to your future occupation. I would advise taking those, or, even better, auditing a course. The information is usually presented in a much smaller room and the subject matter will be geared to either your major or even more specialized than that. The person lecturing will, most likely, have experience in the field you want to enter and may be a very valuable resource even after the course ends. Many classmates of mine hated the business classes we were required to take because they were studying either agriculture or horticulture and had no desire to run a corporation or seek investors. In the business classes for our majors, they were only slightly engaged. Meanwhile, I went into my first business class having already been in business for three years and I quite enjoyed it. We went over the basics of a very complex topic, which was very useful.

Not in a position to be attending college full-time? That is perfectly understandable. There is an untapped resource in community colleges all over the country. Professors who teach business at community colleges have something that most other professors don't - real world experience. The most useful professors are the ones who have done what they teach. They have worked in the business that they are teaching about. They can offer the real world insight into what they are preaching. Community colleges are overlooked by many, but for an entrepreneur, you can learn a lot, make connections, and follow your path at your own pace. Check out your local community college and do some research on classes that might benefit you, from accounting, to marketing, or management, and anything else that you feel you need to keep you moving forward.

During my senior year of college, I decided to take a class called "Introduction to Entrepreneurship," just because. This was a one-credit class taught by two lecturers, who are entrepreneurs. One is a very successful restaurant owner and the other is a not-so-successful video game designer for the blind (a very cool idea that just hadn't taken off). This class was filled with over one-hundred students looking for a professor, who would prance around the auditorium telling them that they could be whatever they wanted to be when they graduate, that whatever business pitch they had, they could sell it. This class was filled with dreamers, and I like people who dream, as without them, we wouldn't have a lot of the cool stuff we have today.

These dreamers took the class very seriously, whereas I did not. I walked into the class thinking that I had all the answers, as I was going into the sixth year of owning my own business. The idea that I would learn from one of these kids who have never had a job, let alone started a business, was beneath me. That week I opened a fortune cookie that said, "Never make the mistake of thinking that you know everything about anything." Crap... the cookie was right. Whether I liked it or not, I had to keep an open mind in the class. So I went almost every week, sat through some pretty interesting elevator pitches, and learned a few things from them. A class like this was designed to give students the opportunity to step out of the box of conventional one-way education. It would be interesting to learn the success rates of the class after graduation, like if they actually do decide to become entrepreneurs or not.

I am often asked, "Can entrepreneurship be taught?" There is ongoing debate about that very question. Can we actively teach students how to be entrepreneurs? It is like asking if you can teach someone to be a politician. There are schools for lawyers, doctors, teachers, but none specifically for entrepreneurs. In our educational system, we are focused on giving students little doses of everything, in order to give them a diversified knowledge base. Think about the dreaded general education requirements in our college system today.

This diversified knowledge base allows students to get a taste of what they will need to know about the world, then to reach further to see where they want to go with it. If you were to walk into a pre-school and start talking about business entities and which one would best suit each child, you would probably get Play-Doh thrown at you. If you are in a college class like the one I took, "Introduction to Entrepreneurship," you will be surrounded by people, who sought out that topic. The class will be receptive to the prospects of entrepreneurship, and the students can be taught all the skills needed to go out and start a business, but not everything can be taught in a classroom. I learned business by doing business. When it comes down to it, what makes entrepreneurs entrepreneurs and everyone else, everyone else? I think that, deep down, there is an entrepreneur inside each of us. It just takes some of us a little longer to discover it.

> *"All humans are entrepreneurs not because they should start companies but because the will to create is encoded in human DNA."*
> — Reid Hoffman

The idea that you aren't smart enough to be an entrepreneur is just another excuse to put off achieving your dream. You will forever be a closet wantrepreneur if you continue to think you are inadequate or unprepared. When I was 16, I may have been young, naive, broke, and a little crazy, but I wasn't applying for early acceptance to Harvard. I started my business, and with every roadblock that caused me to question my ability, I learned, and I continue to learn every day. I surround myself with mentors, who are farmers, small business owners, and bookkeepers, whom I have built relationships with, and can ask for help. If you never ask, you will never know.

CHRISTOPHER GRANT

WHAT OTHER PEOPLE THINK

*"Be who you are and say what you feel,
because those who mind don't matter, and
those who matter don't mind."*
— Dr. Seuss

This quote was probably on your classroom wall in grade school, referring to bullies. Let me tell you, as a wantrepreneur, the thoughts of other people are some of the scariest things you could ever imagine. If your business is still a dream, a vision in your mind, the idea of telling another person may be worse than having a root canal without Novocain.

I can remember the day when I told my parents that I wanted to start a business. I had been walking down the hallway of my high school when my assistant principal asked me to step into his office. He told me the story of how he and his family grew plants for garden centers. He talked about how the business was a way to help put his kids through college, and give them a summer job. I thought he was offering me a job, until he said that the business had been shut down for the past few years. He asked if I wanted the greenhouses. In a few minutes, I had a post-it note with the business information on it.

Like a scene from Charlie & the Chocolate Factory, I rushed home and immediately spilled all of the information to my mother. I was blessed to have one of the best mothers on earth, so she was not going to let her little boy dive into this just yet. I got the classic, "Let's wait and see what dad has to say." Like every young person, I had come to realize that phrases like "We'll see," or "Let me talk it over with Dad," were just ways of putting off the reality that it was never going to happen. This was true of requests for cereal (only for the toy inside), going to a friend's house for a sleepover with no intention of sleeping, and just about every other "Can I?" you can think of.

Like every kid, I knew the lingo and how to play the game. For the rest of the night, I was the best son in the world. I miraculously got all of my homework done in good time, and I even helped with dishes. This was a night my father was working overnight at the fire station, however, so there would be no hope of talking to him until the next evening.

I carefully mapped out my proposal to my father throughout that night and the next school day. Despite my lack of sleep, due to the thousands of thoughts running around in my head, I had my speech down to an inaugural tone. I came home from school hoping that my dad would be there, but I had to wait until 6:15 for him to get out of his other job. Like a parent waiting for his child, who had broken curfew, I remember sitting in the kitchen, pretending to be watching the news, but just waiting for his return. Once he walked in the door, we exchanged the usual greetings and small talk about what the day had thrown our way and if he had gotten any exciting calls at the fire department. Timing was critical. We ate dinner and, like a saint, I helped put things away.

My dad was sitting on his stool watching the news and catching up on the newspaper and mail from the past two days, still in his greasy mechanic's uniform. I started with the classic, "Hey, you'll never guess what happened to me at school yesterday…" and I dumped the day's event of my meeting with the assistant principal and everything we talked about in slurry of ideas to sway his opinion. The display was like nothing I had practiced.

In my mind, I was going to look like a Kennedy captivating the attention of the American people. Yet in a fit of verbal diarrhea, I spilled my soul onto my poor father. He had very little to say. Just a few questions with the dad eyes. The ones asking, "Do you know what you're doing?" His responses were less than satisfying for my energy. I had pictured him jumping in the air with excitement, yet my flustered proposal had left him less than enthusiastic.

I slowed myself down and continued just as I had practiced. It took a while to get my message across. In return, I got, "We can set up a time to meet with him and see what we can do." That was a big golden YES in my book! My mind was, now, going to be busier than ever, because I was going to start a business.

Once the ball was rolling, telling people that I, a 16-year-old, owned a business was not very easy. Everyone thought I just worked for my family business, when it was really the other way around. My parents actually became my first employees, much to their dismay.

We tend to fear the judgment of other people in whatever we do. We worry about the clothes we wear, the car we drive, and even the people with whom we are seen. There is a type of fear wrapped up in what other people think about us. I am sure that when they saw me, 16 years old and running a business, no one really took me seriously. If anything, I am sure people humored me because they thought it was cute. Today I'm 23, and at times, I feel that people still treat me differently than other business owners because of my, relatively, young age. Wouldn't that be considered ageism?

I know that my friends probably talk about me and my crazy ideas behind my back. I am sure even family members talk about what I'm doing with my time and speculating how much money I take in. The competition at farmers' markets talks about me, mainly because they all talk about one another, it is pretty unavoidable. I know that people like to talk and judge others. I also know that most of what is said gets back to me one way or another, whether I like it or not.

I remember hearing once that the hardest part of business is minding your own. There you go - the hardest part about running your business is to not worry about what other people think or say. What other people say behind your back is none of your business. I mean, if they are saying nice things, that's good. If they are saying negative things, that is none of your business. Some people may think you are crazy, starting a business in such tough economic times. Other people might be genuinely worried about you failing. You will find that the people, who judge you the most, are those who are jealous of you. Maybe they are closet wantreprenures themselves who haven't mustered up enough courage to start their own business.

If you constantly worry about what other people are thinking about you and your dream, you will get so caught up in emotions that you will be moving forward just to spite others. If you replace your drive for success with spite, your business will be for nothing. By worrying about others' opinions, you will lose sight of the most important thing - achieving your dream. The day that you are no longer a wantrepreneur, but a full-fledged entrepreneur will be clouded by the negativity of others.

"Why not go out on a limb? That is where the fruit is." - Will Rodgers

As you start to tell people what you are doing, they will fall into a few different groups. There will be those people, who will support you until the cows come home, like family and close friends. There are those who will congratulate you and will remain quiet until you reach some level of success. There will be those people, who do not support you at all, for a whole slew of reasons. The first group, the diehard supporters, will be your biggest asset when starting your business. They will be willing to lend a hand with their own time and skills. For all the negativity in the world, I know that in everyone's life, there will be people, who step up and want to see you succeed. This will take so much of the fear away.

These are the true believers, beyond mom and dad, who come out of the woodwork when you have nothing to pay them with, other than beer and pizza. When people see your ambition and drive, no matter how crazy your idea may have seemed to them at the beginning, your light may have changed them into believers in your dream. So many people want to be a part of something today, to feel like they contributed to something bigger than themselves. Small business start-ups, like yours, are the perfect opportunity for that. I could make a list of all the people who have had my back since day one. They know who they are and they know how much I appreciate them.

When you tell people your dream, and that you are starting a business, many will come back with follow-up questions. A rapid fire of, "How are you doing that?" and "Where are you getting the money?" and all the who, what, when, where, why, and how questions you can think of. Don't be scared!

You have every response to each and every question they throw your way, because as an entrepreneur, you created your business and know everything about it. You will get better at explaining your vision with time. Clear and concise responses keep people interested. If you were to ask me, "So what do you do?" I would respond simply by saying, "I own Grant Family Farm in Essex, Massachusetts, where I grow vegetables, cut flowers, and raise eggs for farmers' markets and wholesalers." This is a much better response than saying, "Ummm, I grow vegetables, weird ones like kohlrabi, and bok choy. I have laying hens for eggs, which we sell at farmers markets and other farms. We also do farmers' markets, and we have cut flowers for sale, too." This is one example of how I've taken my business description from being a slow, one-way conversation to a quick, to-the-point response. I know everything there is to know about my business, because I made it.

You should recognize people whom you admire and with whom you can communicate well. I have always admired my college dean, Bill Mitchell. Bill has an amazing way of making friends with everyone he comes in contact with. When responding to questions, he is clear and concise. His conversations are always based on the other people, asking questions and making connections. Whenever our paths cross, he makes me want to be a better communicator. I'm sure there is someone whom you can try to emulate when talking with people about your business. If you are annoyingly confident and ramble on about everything and anything you can think of regarding your business, they will be put off by that, too.

The best way to become a good conversationalist is to learn from a good conversationalist. If you get nervous talking to people, look for people who are good at it. Then, do what they do, and practice doing what they do throughout your day. The most important habit of being a good conversationalist is to be genuinely interested in others. Most people love talking, and talking about themselves. Go ahead, ask questions, curiosity can help steer you out of the dreaded awkward silence.

Professionalism will be a key factor when telling people about your new venture. When I find myself in a situation where I don't know anyone, I practice responding to questions as if I were being interviewed on TV. I am friendly, concise, and clear with my responses. If the conversation progresses past the basic rapid questions, make sure you are personable and honest, but don't tell them too much. The fact of the matter is, people are nosey.

For instance, when talking to skeptics about your

business, people may bring up money, or casually tell you a number they make, in hopes of you telling them how much you make or have invested. I learned from an old farmer that you will go crazy if you spend your days trying to figure out another farmer. This applies to everyone. People want to know everything. In conversation, keep money and finances to yourself. I have a few innovative projects on my farm and people always try to find out how I make it all work. When you find your secret to success or your groove that works for you, leave that piece of the puzzle out. This will keep people thinking about you.

On the other side of this fear of what others think, is letting yourself get caught up in those businesses that belong to other entrepreneurs. Worrying about competing businesses, and what others have that you don't, will just make you crazy. I've been there. It is very easy to become envious of other established businesses and their market share. I don't have the picturesque farm that is all in one location. I have land all over town, to which I travel. I don't have a force of workers to help me, and I don't have brand new equipment. If I worried about stuff like that, I wouldn't have any time to get any work done. The hardest part of business is minding your own.

People talk, and as you become involved with trade organizations or entrepreneur groups, you'll find that people love to talk about the good, but more so the bad. If you spend all your time worrying about what other people are doing or saying, you will never get your business off the ground. The most important thing to worry about is you and your business. Make sure you take pride when it comes to talking about your business. I am bashful and don't like to sound like I'm bragging, so I sometimes undermine my unique way of doing things. There is a line between being professionally proud of your dream and accomplishments and being cocky about them. At times, I still worry about what people are thinking or saying about me. I think that is hard wired into us, but every day I practice minding my own business, because that is all I can really handle.

NEW IMAGE

I know that, as a young entrepreneur, I am always looked at a little differently than most. I'm sure, at first, some thought I was cute and they gave me some leeway. Others really wanted to see me succeed. I've attended many of the hundreds of trade shows that are related to the green industry around the country. Many people, who will attend them, go to the local or regional conference to see the new products or hear a speaker, but mainly they go to get out of the house because the majority of them are laid off during the off season.

So there I was, brand new Grant's Plants t-shirt on, clean hat, ready to take on the little trade show hosted by my hard goods supplier. I was seventeen years old, drove just over two hours to get there, and, like any other seventeen-year-old, who drives that far from home, I brought my mom. We picked up our name badges and started walking around the booths. There was everything from bagged soil to plugs and cutting suppliers were there lining up orders for the spring. I was perusing the aisles with my mom by my side.

Every salesman would look at me, then look at my

mother, then give us the trade show pickup line, "Have you ever used our…." followed by the product or service. My mother was a professional quilter and house painter, she knew very little about plants or what I did or did not use. She was there for moral support and to grab every pen, pencil, pad of paper, ruler, and piece of candy she could get from these people. After the slick sales person dropped the pickup line of their choice on my mother, she would look at them and say, "Talk to him, I've got nothing to do with this" or 'Hey Chris, do we use this stuff?"

The salesperson would look at me and then take on a whole new personality, as if I was wasting their time, as I would tell them that "I have not bought plants from you because we do not grow tropical plants" or "Yes, we already grow with MetroMix potting soil and have never had a problem with it."

I had one mission that day - to talk to a certain supplier of sheet pots. In any catalog, if you sell pots and picture them in a tray, you obviously need to show the correct tray for the pots. Yet I was sold die-cut sheet pots and given directions to put them in a standard 1020 tray. I came to find out that the sheets fit just fine in the trays, but when transported, my plants shifted, accordion-like. The catalog had shown a tray that locked in with the sheet pots, but the customer service woman, I had spoken with, had assured me that the company did not make them. I went to the booth that housed the manufacturer of the pots and waited. I was in no rush, as the salesperson was talking with another customer. So I waited.

Twenty minutes later, after a hunt for some "good pens," my mother found me still standing at the booth. My mom started wandering around the display of pots and trays. The vendor looked up from talking to the other customer and said, "Ma'am, I will be with you in just a moment." I was born with patience, but this was really pushing it. He finished with the clients and walked over to my mom. When asked how he could help her, she pointed at me.

Finally, he noticed I was holding the display sample of the pots I bought from the catalog, and the trays that matched them. When he asked, "What can I help you with?" I was less than impressed with his attitude. I explained the whole fiasco with the distributor and how they had said they didn't make trays for these pots. He responded with, "Well, they're right here," like I was trying to prove to him that they did not make them! I responded with, "Sir, I can see that, but how can I get twelve more cases of these trays to my house?" The man wrote up an order and said that they'd be there within two weeks.

Looking back, I understand that there are very few wholesale buyers, who are seventeen, but it taught me great lesson in customer service. Every customer is important, whether they buy $100,000 or $500 worth of product each year. You never know where people will end up in life, so treat everyone like they buy $100,000 worth of product even if they only buy $500. If you do, when they do start buying $100,000 you will already have their business.

When you start out you will be looked at with all kinds of assumptions, whether you're young, old, tattooed, ears pierced, or have hair dyed neon yellow. Sadly, everyone judges a book by its cover. When you think about your professional image within your industry, don't shoot for just acceptable. Because we all care so much about appearance, you should carry yourself with the kind of professionalism expected in that industry. Working in the field of agriculture, I don't wear a suit to go plant beans, but when it comes to trade shows and other meetings, I dress appropriately. When you begin going to industry meetings, you will learn that those, who walk into a room in jeans and Tevas, sit with a little different crowd than those, who wear industry-appropriate clothing. This will vary by industry, but even at a vegetable growers convention, we don't dress like we just fell off the turnip wagon.

When dealing with the public, if you know your industry, you will know how to dress. If you are a hairdresser, you will dress as hairdressers dress. If you are a technology entrepreneur, you will know how those in the technology field dress. I am not telling you to give up your

Birkenstocks for a pair of boat shoes or anything drastic, but when trying to project an image of professionalism to the world, you will have to play the part. You can only make a first impression once.

They say that the world is run by those who show up. I said, "they say," because the author is disputed, so whoever said this line, I thank you. It is true that the world is run by those who show up, so I have learned to show up. My advice to you: show up, show up early and bring snacks. Wherever you are going, meeting, trade show, event, make sure you show up early, because no one likes it when people are late. Bring snacks? Yes, bring snacks, because if you are late, no one can be mad at the guy or gal, who brings doughnuts or a bag of mini candy bars to a meeting, late or not. If it is an event, bring snacks, because you have no idea when the meal will be served or how long the speaker will go for. There you have it, my secret to success, show up early and bring snacks.

Showing up is so important when you are trying to make a name for yourself. If you are entering a new industry where you know practically no one or you are starting a new business in a related industry where you know many people, make sure you show up. I attend meetings all over New England about flowers, vegetables, bugs, poultry, food safety, government relations, public policy, small business owners, and others that spark an interest, because I intend to be known as the one who shows up. This is important in such a busy time, where every minute of my day is valuable.

What is even more valuable is being asked to join a board or committee, because you always show up and are involved in a small way. Showing up shows that you care and you are enthusiastic about the topic. This will help you gain knowledge, connections, and stature in your industry, even if you are new to the game.

There are hundreds of groups and trade organizations that you can join, and they can all help you network. Take time to find what ones suit you the best and try them out. I will warn you, you may get stretched too thin if you become overly involved in trade groups, so budget your time wisely so you do not become burnt out early. Also, make sure you do not approach every organization with the attitude that you will be president within a year. Tight knit organizations will be less likely to take you in and show you around if you are cocky and start making the scene all about you. Be careful.

As a twenty-something, I am conditioned to using email, texting, and Facebook as forms of communication. I want you to know that real business gets done when you pick up the phone. The vast majority of decision makers in business still pick up the phone, meet clients for lunch, and follow up with a Christmas card. To some, this is old school, but to most this is how it is done. I have many entrepreneur friends, who will say that they have been waiting for someone to email them back for days. When I ask if they tried to call them, they look at me like I have three heads.

One specific example is a friend, who was waiting for a confirmation from a customer to purchase a load of materials, along with another order. The customer didn't responded, so I made him pick up the phone and call. Was the customer mad? No! He thanked my friend repeatedly for calling to confirm. The customer had seen the email, but as some of us do, just keep scrolling, and he didn't responded. All you have to do is pick up the phone, and things get done.

You shouldn't judge a book by its cover, even though most people do

Starting out, how do you want to look? You have the opportunity to create the image you want to project to the world about you and your new enterprise. I think you know that you can only make one first impression, so you might as well make it a good one. When you are using a bubblegum and duct tape budget, your image will be a grass roots one. You might not have the resources, funny term for money, to make your image exactly how you dreamed from day one. I do not have the picturesque farm that I dreamed of when I started, because I am working with what I have, my family's land.

Do not get me wrong, I love it here. When you think of a classic New England farm, you picture a red barn, ours is yellow. My image is not perfect but it is evolving. I have a logo, fonts, color schemes, that keep all of my business' image coherent and constant. I present myself well at farmers markets, meetings, and anywhere else I come in contact with customers, new and old. Consistency in your message, business style, and manor will all create a solid image. You might not be able to rent a giant office, on day one, with a receptionist with a fancy headset, but one day you might. Just because it is not in the budget today, doesn't mean your dream image can't be reality down the road. You will be amazed what you will find down the road, you just have to keep moving.

Proving the world wrong isn't a life goal.

A life goal should be to find something you love doing, finding who you belong with, working hard, believing in yourself, and pushing yourself far beyond what is expected of you.

If you do all that, you will have a fulfilled life... And proving the world wrong will be a happy byproduct.

MONEY

Growing up, I was blessed to be taught the value of a dollar. We were lucky enough to live on the farm on which my dad worked. Part of the payment was being able to live in the house on the farm. He was paid at the beginning of every month. With three kids and a wife, by the end of the month, money was tight. When I was young, I was aware that we didn't have as much money as other families in town - by the old Chevy Blazer my mom drove, the hand-me-downs and handmade clothes we wore, and the fact that we never really went out to eat.

Growing up, I think we all knew that we were different, but we were happy. When we were old enough, my mom took on part-time jobs, and when the farm was sold, my dad became a full-time firefighter. We bought the house I grew up in, and have been working hard to keep it ever since. Growing up in a thrifty house gave me a sort of fear about money. Financial insecurity is always on my mind. I was probably the most fiscally responsible fourth-grader you could know, when I got my first paper route. As other kids dropped their routes, I picked up their customers until I was delivering to half of my small town. The fear of poverty and the pride of working hard that my parents instilled in us has made us kids surprisingly fiscally responsible as we grew up.

> *"Security is mostly a superstition, it does not exist in nature... Life is either a daring adventure or nothing."* — Helen Keller

Financial obligations are a legitimate fear when starting a business. Something that I am frequently asked about in my business is money. Where did I get the money to start my business? At 16 years old, venture capitalists were not chasing my school bus. I used my own savings to get the business up and running. I like to call this the "bubblegum and duct tape budget."

Depending on the scope of the business that you are starting, my advice is to always start small and slow, because that's really all you can do. Great things take time to evolve. Remember how Rome was built? There are a lot of sources from which to get money - family, friends, banks, venture capitalists, the government. As a young person, selling your golden idea, no matter how outstanding it is, is difficult. Your credibility as a business owner is little to none. I have always been wary about borrowing money, because of the sheer fact that at some point or another, you have to give it back, plus interest. Asking Grandma for a large sum of money can be uncomfortable, scary, and sometimes inappropriate or insulting to some people. Money is a touchy subject for many people, even between some married couples.

I know most people want to put all the chips they have on the table and go big or go home, but as a wantrepreneur, you should really ask for guidance on this one. Budgeting your income and savings so that you can start a business on the side can be tricky. I recommend consulting with a bookkeeper or an accountant, who can help you figure out what you can afford to invest in your dream. This guidance can be powerful, but also disheartening. They may recommend saving for a while or using finances from your other investments.

It is all dependent on your specific situation. Bubblegum and duct tape budgets are the key to success. Knowing where your money is coming from, usually your own funds, and using it creatively will pay off. This is the grassroots of entrepreneurship. The cookie-cutter dream of investors hunting you down or loan officers waving money at you, most likely isn't going to happen. Down the road, you may find yourself in a position to take on investors or get loans. When that happens, I will be the first to applaud you! At the beginning, while you are still a wantrepreneur, money is a scary and valuable subject.

As a grass roots, bootstrap, bubblegum and duct tape entrepreneur, I have been known to go over budget. I would have to supplement my budget with some of my own money. This became more and more prevalent throughout college, because college was expensive. I would float myself a loan from the odd jobs I worked in the winter. I was making sure I didn't run out of money, when I really should have stopped spending all of it. Crazy idea, don't spend money if you don't have any.

You will want to keep inching your bank account along to keep the business afloat. That is a dangerous game my friend. I know that you would do anything in the world to make your dream work out, believe me, I've been there. This kind of spending can only go on for so long. One of the biggest reasons businesses fail is that they are underfunded. That is true, because it is expensive to be your own boss and create something out of a dream. Your bookkeeper can tell you that you are on a slippery slope, especially if you are draining your own personal bank account. Budget, budget, budget your spending.

For instance, you do not need 500 t-shirts with your company logo on it for your closest friends, even if your shirts are wicked cool and say "Get fresh with a local farmer" on the back. I fear running out of money all the time, especially in the spring, when the farm starts up again. It is so tempting to fall back into footing the bill, but you have to keep in mind that at some point your business will have to float on its own, or you will not be able to afford the bill yourself. Unless you are a millionaire, then float away. There is a trick to making a small fortune farming. The key is to start with a very large fortune.

Today, as social media consumes more and more of our everyday lives, the advent of crowd funding has opened many doors for entrepreneurs, who need help funding their startup. Crowd funding websites are portals through which you can open an account, set up a profile and goal, attach a video about your goal, and have people pledge money to you. The idea is simple - the digital grassroots effort to fund a goal. There are a few more steps.

The beneficiary of the money will only receive the amount if the full amount of money is raised by the deadline. These campaigns only last for a set amount of time, running indefinitely would potentially lessen the excitement for people to fire up their computers and pledge. Each donor is entitled to a prize in return based on the amount of money they pledge if the beneficiary meets their deadline. Gifts for donors vary depending on a few factors (the nature of the business, the size of the business, how much a donor gives), and are only rewarded if the deadline is met.

The owner of a small bakery, who wants to buy a new oven may set a goal for $5,000. The first level gift may be a hand-written thank you note and a voucher for a free cookie. The second level may get a hand-written thank you note and a voucher for a dozen free cookies. The third level may get a hand-written thank you note and a voucher for a free personalized cookie cake for your next birthday, and so on. The incentives are not why people donate money to crowd funding sites and businesses that they might not even know, but they help sweeten the pot.

Crowd funding has been successful because people want to feel like they can help, even if it is just taking the time to enter their credit card information to give $25. This platform gives you the opportunity to get the message out there that you are doing something new, fun, innovative, and you need their help. The power of social media is limitless and you should take advantage of it every chance you get. There are a few crowd funding websites like Kickstarter, Indiegogo, and Crowdfunder.

I have never used crowd funding personally, but there are countless stories of successful campaigns that have helped entrepreneurs move forward to the next level with the help of this digital grassroots platform. I recommend researching the rules, success rates, and problems with each of the crowd funding platforms that are out there. When I look for issues or downfalls with a product or service I simply Google the name of the company or product and "issues," "problems," or "bad reviews." You can also search websites like the Better Business Bureau to see consumer reviews on each. Weigh your options when choosing a platform; then make sure you look into what makes a successful campaign reach its funding goal.

Take the time to model your campaign after those that had a similar goal, and try contacting the business to see if they have any insight. I wouldn't advise that you craft a campaign to get yourself a new sports car to impress clients, but build it around something that would be a game changer for your business, and be genuine.

Investors aren't just the people, who can offer you money. As an entrepreneur, you will have to start calling in all the favors you are owed in order to get the business off the ground. There are people in your life, who will be willing to lend a hand doing whatever they can. These people will invest their time, skills, and support into your business when you can't even pay them. Why would anyone waste their time helping you? Unless you are making your investors work like they are full-time employees, asking for help can really pay off, even if you are paying them in pizza, beer, or the services you offer. How could you use these time investors?

Attending farmers' markets is more than a one-man job. It takes two, maybe three, people to make my little stand run. At the beginning, I couldn't afford to really hire someone to help sell my products. I enlisted the help of my Aunt Diane and grandmother to help me at the farmers' markets. How do I pay them? In vegetables, eggs, and cut flowers. If you put it out there, to your friends and family, that you need help, you will be surprised how willing people are to lend a hand. You won't be getting a 40-hour-a-week employee for free or trade, but maybe a few hours a week you can use them where you need the most help. I will remind you to be grateful for all of the help you receive from these time investors. They will become some of your most valuable assets.

Believe me, I am stubbornly independent when it comes to my business and my life. I do not like working with people, because I know I can get it done my way. You will quickly learn that if you try and do everything yourself, your little business world will become incredibly difficult. This is what I consider working inside the box. When I started out, I wanted to do it all on my own, especially when it came to graphic design and web design. I didn't need any fancy graphic designer to make a logo or code a website, I could do it all by myself. I did just that, I bought a logo design program for my computer and signed up for a template website. I filled in the content of the web pages, and even before I read it twice I released it to the world. I told everyone via text and Facebook to go look at my website! Come to find out, I was not very good at writing web content. The design template I chose was slow and not very welcoming. The grammar and spelling errors throughout the page were downright embarrassing. I learned something from that experience, buying a cheap website and doing it cheap, made me look cheap. I am not a website developer, I am a farmer.

As far as that logo design program, I still have it, it is here on my laptop, only been opened twice. After it didn't have the font I really wanted or any of the images

I wanted, I gave up. I learned quickly that I am not a graphic designer. Once again, I am a farmer.

I didn't just tell you this to point out that I am stubborn, but to let you know that no matter what, there are times that you are going to have to ask for help. I know, I know, you are an entrepreneur not a third grader (or maybe you are). At the beginning, you can find those friends that build web pages to help get you off the ground and some students that work in graphic design looking for extra money. I have utilized both. There will come a time that you will need a professional website and high-quality graphic design work done, and you are going to have to hire someone. This sounds scary, but I learned that it is easier than you think.

The world has this group of people, who call themselves freelancers. These are professionals, who have skills ranging from editing, graphic design, app designers, ghostwriters, web developers, the list goes on. Freelancers usually have day jobs in their respected fields, but do work on the side for additional income. How do you get in touch with freelancers? You can use websites like elance.com.

You can post a job on Elance with a description of the work you need done, how much you are willing to pay, hourly or for the entire job, and the due date. Freelancers will bid on the job, and you can review their proposal and qualifications to see who fits best for your job and budget.

Freelancers that use sites like Elance range in experience from college age students to high profile editors, who work in large publishing houses to people with Ph.Ds in your field. They all have the same opportunity to bid on your project. You select the best match for you, fund the project via Elance, and they work with you under the terms of the proposal until completed, you accept the job, and pay the freelancer.

Sounds simple, but here are some things you might need to look out for. If you are having someone edit, make sure they are native speakers of your language, because anyone in the world with a computer bid and deliver less that desirable results. Look at the freelancers previous work, ratings, and reviews. Always pay and communicate through the Elance portal for the most secure transaction. Give good reviews of successful jobs and go back to the freelancer if you like their work. If the job isn't completed, that is OK, you choose another freelancer and you keep moving. Make sure you read the terms of the site you choose, as there are others such a guru.com and freelancer.com. Elance is only one example of may platforms that you can use.

How much do freelancers cost? It all depends on who you hire. A simple digitalization of a logo idea could be done for under $50. A line edit of a 40,000 word manuscript can range from $35 to $2,500. It all depends on your budget, but I will give you a hint, you will pay for quality.

Freelancers are great because you are not hiring them as a payroll employee. They handle all of the financial logistics. Most are experts in their fields and are willing to help. Some freelancers you hire you will never meet in person, because they are from all over the world, no need to go to an office or travel. I have never met any of my freelancers face to face. I have had good results with freelancers, others have had not so great results, you will have to take the good with the bad. Hiring freelancers is one way that I can alleviate my workload. I post small jobs and have them done lightening fast with great results. No need to hire an ad agency to develop your business logo or other designs when you are bootstrapping your dream, you can get it done on your budget, with a little help.

"If you want to go fast, go alone. If you want to go far, go together." — African Proverb

I know that I can't be good at everything. In fact I would rather be great at one thing, instead of mediocre at a thousand things. I am not a tax specialist, graphic designer, marathon runner, or editor. I am a farmer. When it comes to taxes, graphic design, running a marathon, or editing, I seek help from professionals. My editors always have a field day working with my wicked good New England grammar and sentence structure. I know what I am good at. What I cannot learn to do well and enjoy, I leave for the professionals.

I hired multiple freelancers to create this book like editors, page designers, and the cover designer. I trust them and their professionalism to deliver quality work. That being said, I will ask for your help. Due to my endless pursuit of perfection, if you happen to find an error, please drop me an e-mail at: lookwhoisntperfect@ fearsofawantrepreneur.com (crazy e-mail address I know). If you are one of the first people to spot an error, I will send you a little gift. When I receive critiques, I will go back in the book and fix them for future readers. This is me asking for help.

My parents had very little training when it came to business administration, so I was referred to a family friend, who was a bookkeeper, Jodi. I remember our first meeting like I was addressing Congress. Normally I am a fairly fluent speaker, yet this time, in our meeting, I could not talk in anything but a monotone. I was so afraid that my ideas would get compromised for some reason or even worse, shot down. We talked for about an hour about what I wanted to do and how to bring my bank statements to her on time. That was the key, bring them to her office on time. I must have been shaking like a leaf, sitting across from her in that chair looking out at the marsh behind her.

This meeting was only the second time I had ever told anyone about my business idea or my dream. Jodi is many things to me - a great sounding board, the voice of reason and business savvy - but she is also anything but brief. I will go to drop off statements, and it turns into an hour-long conversation about kale marketing. She has become one of my greatest supporters over the years. When I receive a letter from the IRS, rather than opening it, I instantly call her. Her sense of humor and wit have gotten me through hard times, even times when I wanted to throw it all away. I bring a list of goals at the beginning of each year to her. This book was on it, and it was one of the only goals she kind of laughed at, because she knows just how busy I am. These are the relationships that keep you going, even in the darkest of times.

I am sure you want me to tell you what kind of entity that you should start your business as, or what kind of permits and licenses you need for your business, but that would take so much time, and I am not an expert in giving such advice. My advice is to start that conversation with business owners you know and trust. Trust is the key. Start the dialog with a bookkeeper or accountant about what you need if you do not already know.

The people at your local Chamber of Commerce are full of information that can help you get on your way to business. I know that in my area the Chamber of Commerce offers free small business consulting with real business owners. This is an amazing opportunity for a new entrepreneur, because the knowledge you gain is not from a text book, but the real world and the relationships you build are critical to networking.

Another resource that I use is the U.S. Small Business Administration. The Small Business Administration or SBA is a governmental agency that is dedicated to helping the American small business. The www.sba.gov is packed with information and tools for small business owners to start building their infrastructure. The SBA also has local and regional field offices that can assist you. The largest selling point for the SBA is that they are not trying to sell you anything! When you use their services, they are free! This is a great source for unbiased information when it comes to managing a business, whereas other websites may be selling you their philosophy and products.

The Small Business Administration and Chamber of Commerce are two resources that are underutilized, but their information and expertise is invaluable, especially when you are on the duct tape, bubblegum, and ramen-noodle-every-night, budget.

When it comes down to money and achieving your dreams, I believe Stephen Bennett said it the best:

> *"If you do it for the money, that's only what you get."*
> — Stephen Bennett

If you set out to start a business to get rich, you may get that. If you set out to help people or make life easier, better, and more enjoyable for people, you will get all that in return. You will only get what you give. If you give your heart and soul, I hope that you get that in return. Starting a business for the sake of becoming a millionaire is a lofty goal, but then again, when I was writing my essays for college scholarships, one of my main points was that I'm was going to college to learn about vegetable production. Unlike all of the other college freshmen, who had sexy majors like microbiology, political science, or international business, I was honest when I told them I wasn't planning on making a million dollars a year, and I was okay with that. I wanted to go to school to learn about something that I love and that I have a passion for. I would rather be happy than rich.

I asked my bookkeeper once, "Jodi, what was your first impression when I came to you and told you I wanted to start a business?" She said, "Wow, a kid, who knows what he wants to do with his life, is passionate about it, and is going to make it happen." She believed in me, because I had a plan and believed in myself. I followed with another question asking her, "Why haven't you told me to close up and get a real job?" She responded saying, "You don't strike me as the kind of person, who would put money before passion for something." People like Jodi are the reason I can keep doing what I love. In this crazy world, there are still people out there, who want to see others succeed. There are still good people in the world that are willing to go with you on a journey, even if it doesn't end in fame and fortune.

That is an ideal answer from a naïve twenty-something, but I also think it's a legitimate goal. Wherever you are in your life, money should not be the deciding factor when it comes to accomplishing your goals and dream of owning a business. If you want to go from being a wantrepreneur to an entrepreneur, your drive and creativity will play a huge role in how you handle your finances from day one.

There is no shame in asking for help. You will be amazed at all the doors that open for you; all you have to do is knock.

CHANGE

The business that I started when I was 16 was a wholesale perennial company, and when I started out, I thought that was what I wanted to do forever. Once again, I was only 16. Thinking back, what right-minded, 16-year-old dreams of creating a perennial ground cover empire? This one did. I continued to grow each summer, producing more plants, and adding more customers to my base. The business was growing, but not exactly returning enough profit for that amount of work.

The week before I turned 21, I fell into a slump. I was so bogged down by the greenhouse business that I began making myself sick. This was on top of a pile of family stuff going on at the same time (life happens). I remember lying on the living room floor, defeated. My mom, sitting on the couch, asked me what was wrong and how she could help. I had made so many changes to my plan, that the dream of my plant business had become something that didn't even feel like my own anymore. I had made concessions and had changed to fit the standard, instead of setting it. I was bored with what my business had become - ordinary. Just another plant wholesaler trying to make it in a recession. It was in the middle of my big planting push, and I couldn't stand the thought of continuing my madness. That is when my mom asked me, "What do you want to do? What makes you most happy?"

I said, "The vegetables and chickens."

And for one of the first times, she said with pride, "Then that's what we are going to do. Grow vegetables and raise chickens, and I'll help."

We finished planting that night, and sold off the inventory. Since then, I have drifted away from the greenhouse business, and really stuck to my passion of growing vegetables and raising chickens. At 20 years old, I had had a mid-life crisis. I had hit a wall and needed to be pulled out of my funk and truly reminded about why I was even in business in the first place: to do what I loved, my way.

I didn't sell off the business, because the only tangible parts of it were the greenhouse structures and…me. I started shifting my focus to re-shaping my business to what I really wanted to do - farm. That is when I started looking at farmers' markets and other outlets through which to sell produce. I never thought that I would find that day, but I was tired of working hard on a job I no longer enjoyed, and getting so little back. The idea wasn't far-fetched; I could return to perennial production one day, but at the time, it wasn't in my plan.

I wanted to point out that what had just happened would fall into the category of failure for most. I started the business and ended the business in a five-year period. I didn't turn my back on it, as though it had never happened. Grant's Plants was the best business class I could ever have signed up for. Unlike sitting in a lecture hall, all of the lessons I learned were hands-on. The mistakes I made were real, not just scenarios. The mistakes I made also cost me time and money. When mistakes begin to cost you your own money, you begin learning a lot faster than if you were spending someone else's money.

The years I spent learning from my business gave me so much to take to beginning my newly-formed Grant Family Farm. I didn't take a break to work full-time elsewhere. It was a smooth transition over two years to phase out one business and begin the next. I will be honest, people in my family and in town will probably refer to me and my business as Grant's Plants until I die. I look back and think about the day I told my parents, talked to my accountant for the first time, cut my first big check, and bought a one-million-dollar insurance policy, all before I entered college. Thinking about teenage me, going for it with blinders on, is one lesson that keeps me going today. I use lessons from my first business every day. I will never forget those times that my mind was so wrapped up in my business problems, but in reality, the problems weren't big at all.

I will say that, although some would consider my first business a failure, I consider it a stepping stone. As a great inventor once said:

"I failed my way to success."
— Thomas Edison

Yes, failure and defeat are hard to accept, but if you are anything like me, you can do it. If my business fails tomorrow, then the day after that I will head down to town hall and establish another business, and keep trying. That is what makes you an entrepreneur: the ability to get back up when things get you down.

"The only constant in life is change."
— Francois de La Rochefoucauld

When we finally accept that the only thing in life that remains constant is change, we will be able to loosen up our grip and let things take their course. Now, I am a control freak. Not in the way that I will grab the wheel from the passenger seat when someone else is driving, but I like to know that things are getting done, well, my way. I used to be very caught up in details and making sure things were just right. I learned to ask myself one question, "How important is it?"

If I continue to worry and control every tiny aspect of my business, it would consume my entire life. The business is expanding to the point that I simply cannot control every single detail. I am practicing delegating to others and not micromanaging them. This is the kind of change that I have to deal with in order to expand and grow. That is an important way that I am changing myself to allow other changes to happen. As a farmer, I cannot control the weather. I do my best to work with the weather, rather than against it. I do this by planning and being flexible with the timing of the plan. I can't make it rain, but I can add water to some crops to keep them alive. I also can't cover the fields with an umbrella when we get too much rain, but I can make sure my drainage ditches work before it starts to rain. This all goes back to the idea that, if this was easy, everyone would be doing it, and we would be out of business.

Change is inevitable, but it can also be a huge window of opportunity. When I decided to dissolve my first business, I knew that I still had a passion for growing things. At that time, the local food movement was growing, and still is. I was able to shift my focus as a farmer to fill that niche. Each situation or "curveball" that comes your way can be looked at in a couple of different ways. You can see a change in your market, such as customers starting to back off your product, and throw your hands in the air and say, "Well, we tried. Shut it down."

Or you can do your grassroots research to stay ahead of the curve and find creative ways to keep your business moving forward. If you plan to start your venture and never do anything different, you will become stagnant and you won't get very far. Changing is all a part of life and business. In order to go from being a wantrepreneur to an entrepreneur, you should embrace change as a challenge, instead of a burden.

If you are still a wantrepreneur filled with ideas on how your business will be when it's all in motion, you shouldn't fear the fact that things change. The world is constantly changing, the challenge is to change with it. I can never gauge week-to-week the demand that there will be for certain crops at farmers' markets, so I change week-to-week by one or two degrees. Not a 180-degree shift in what I bring, but just enough to meet the demand for some products and lessen the amount of others. You will have to continually evaluate your market, because if you see that your target market is changing, you will have to make the change with them, or find another niche entirely.

Fearing change can only last so long. The time will come when you are an entrepreneur, when you will be making decisions that will, each time you make them, change the direction of your business. Small adjustments in your trajectory will ultimately change your destination or goals. Think of a tanker or cruise ship. The captain has, in mind, the destination port long before they get there. These behemoth boats are slow to start and slow to turn. If the captain of the boat doesn't stay true to the course they lay out, each wave that comes along will knock them off course little by little.

In the ocean, millions of waves will come before a ship,

and a storm or two will really try to knock the vessel off course. The captain and crew are constantly dealing with the shift, compensating for each wave and storm, to get where they want to be. If they get knocked off their plan just an inch, their final destination will be wrong. When you start out, stick to your plan, but with all the obstacles and curveballs that are thrown at you, you may have to take a detour or even back up and try again. No business is so perfectly cut-and-dry that they can avoid any trial and error. You will have to be creative to stay true to your dream and still attend to all the other factors that play into your business being successful.

"I have not failed, I've just found 10,000 ways that won't work" – Thomas A. Edison

It took Thomas Edison over 10,000 attempts in order to develop the light bulb. Picture his office, filled with every design imaginable, the bulbs and filaments piling up, surrounding him with failure after failure. Each design, slightly different than the last, until it worked. If Edison had given up at 9,999 there is no telling how we would be lighting the world today.

But will it work out?

I love talking over business ideas with people. I have a group of friends, with whom I do it all the time. We talk all the ideas out, determining the problems and possibilities of each. Will it work? That is one question we can't answer until one of us starts that business. You won't know if you don't try. A high school teacher of mine had a sticker on his desk that said, "If you don't shoot, you can't score. If you can't score, you'll never win."

Mr. Vanikiotis was not your average teacher. He is a quiet man, with a lot of knowledge and experience when it comes to having a job that you love. He has worked as a museum exhibit designer, carpenter, boat launch operator, and now a teacher. He tells his students not to worry about money, that if you are doing something you love, money will come. It is a scary thought, to just trust that money will come. He went from making a six-figure salary in the museum business to starting his own business building fences. Why? Why on earth would he leave such a lucrative job?

He wanted to see if he could do it. Mr. V wanted to prove to himself and his family that he could turn his hobby, construction, into a successful business. Within a year, the business had turned a profit and he loved what he did. When it became work for him and he stopped having fun, he gave his half of the business away to his partner and became a teacher.

Why not just grin and bear it? Why not just keep running the company that was making him money? He wasn't having fun, and he had already proven that he could start a business and turn a profit within two years. He plans to retire from teaching in a few years and start another business, this time making furniture. Mr. V is a modest man when he talks about himself, but when he talks about business, he becomes very animated. He loves to see his students move on to find careers doing something that they have a passion for. He taught me to never stop reaching for the next step, because nothing good is ever handed to you. If you don't try, you will never know. This isn't just about starting a business, but about achieving anything in life.

> *"If you don't shoot, you can't score. If you can't score, you'll never win."* — George Vanikiotis

(A quote that is still on his desk today)

Learn to take the Good with the Bad

Once you are in business, I hope you enjoy the ride. There are times when you will run your bank account down to the last few dollars, make decisions to scale back, get stretched too thin, or make a mistake. This is all part of the ride. Some days won't be all bright and cheery; there are events that will throw you off course and circumstances that will make you feel helpless. You will stay up late thinking about all of the stuff you need to get done, and be too tired to do it the next day. It is all part of the ride. This is the path less traveled. It's not easy, but I hope you know that it's worth every minute.

I hope you enjoy the little victories as you move closer and closer to making your dream a reality - the first day you open your storefront, set up your business checking account, land your first big customer, or see your logo printed on a vehicle. These are the times that make being an entrepreneur so great. I hope you love your business the way I love mine.

I made Mr. V a promise when I was in high school. When the day comes that I don't laugh, smile, or love my job, and it becomes work, I will find a new one. If that day comes for you, I hope you take his advice. Take the good with the bad, and enjoy the fact that, as an entrepreneur, you chose the road less traveled.

There is no way that, as a fresh entrepreneur, you can be "on" all the time. I mean there is no way that you can give 100% of yourself without running out of steam, getting bogged down, and falling into a rut. There will be times that you will feel like nothing is going right the world is against you no matter how hard you try. When the world you built is off track, and there is no way to pick it back up and set it right again, and that is when you need your group of supporters. I have a handful of friends that I can call or text that will whip me back into shape. Sometimes it is as simple as them saying in a sarcastic voice, "Come on, you are Chris Grant, mildly successful businessman," and that's all it takes. Sometimes you just have to step out of the situation and look at the problem from a different prospective, and then you see that it's not that bad.

When I need to pull myself out of a bad mood, I often use YouTube. I will simply type in "epic fails," "people falling down stairs," "babies laughing," or "motivational speeches." You will find lots of content on these topics, enough that you could watch videos for days. I've found that a few minutes watching compilations of people falling down stairs, skateboard accidents, or babies laughing like hyenas, puts me in a totally different mindset. Some may say that watching a grown man, rollerblading down a flight of stairs in a park and falling three-quarters of the way down, is morbid.

My rationale behind this is, *he must be OK if his friends put the video on YouTube and it just goes to show that other people might be having a worse day than you.* I have told people this simple trick, sometimes even sending a link via email to help them get in a better mood. That's just the kind of friend I am. You can learn a lot from great speakers on YouTube, from historical speeches to college graduations to movies made specifically to motivate you out of your slump.

When you feel bogged down and you are looking for your exit strategy, don't give up too fast. If you are worried about when your next check will come in, get on the phone. If you are down about how little response you got from your yellow page ad, fire up your laptop and work social media. If you are thinking that starting a business would be like an episode of *The Office* and all you have to do is shuffle paperwork and goof off with co-workers, you will be disappointed.

Starting a business is more like the episode of *I Love Lucy*, the one when they work in the chocolate factory and the conveyor belt moves too fast for them to handle, or to cite more of a modern analogy, the show *Shark Tank* when billionaires shoot down entrepreneurs, who are looking for funding. Sometimes they invest, but man can they be mean. Do not make split second decisions when you are in a bad place, because as they say "This too shall pass."

> *"Never cut a tree down in the wintertime. Never make a negative decision in the low time. Never make your most important decision when you are in your worst moods. Wait. Be patient. The storm will pass. The spring will come."*
> — Robert H. Schuller

LUCK

Luck and fate are some of things that people blame for their position in life. So many people fill their heads with the idea that they are unlucky, or they were destined to be something less. This idea that the universe is out to get them can only last so long before people give up trying and settle. You have to play the hand that you are dealt, no matter how bad it may seem. Whatever you are given in life, work with it, make something out of what you have when you have it. If you develop the notion that there are many people in the world that have it better off than you, and that is all you see, that is all you will ever believe. Here is where the touchy-feely comes into play. If you tell a lie enough times, it eventually becomes the truth, or becomes believed as though it is true.

If you continue to wake up every morning and believe that you are unlucky or your fate is to be miserable, that is exactly what will happen. To own a business you cannot be a pessimist. You won't make it very far.

I was a sophomore in high school, when I was taking the late bus home from school. There was a girl on the bus, who had never taken that specific bus or seen where I lived. As we came around the corner and I was grabbing my belongings, she said, "You live there?" I smiled and said, "Yes." The girl responded, "Wow you are so lucky, your parents must be rich or something." The joke was on her. My parents aren't rich, and luck has nothing to do with it. My parents and aunt and uncle work hard to keep our house and farm. Our property is, in my opinion, one of the most beautiful places in the world. We were lucky that we had the opportunity to buy the land, but have worked hard to keep it.

> *"I've always worked very, very hard, and the harder I worked, the luckier I got."*
> – Alan Bond

So many people blame their upbringing and experiences for not being able to move forward and accomplish goals. People believe that their circumstances and past must dictate their future. If you were brought up in a bad family, you can change. If you come from a long line of addicts in your family, you can change. If you were an orphan, grew up in a bad part of town, didn't get good grades in school, got involved with a bad group of friends, dropped out of school, had a child at a young age, or can't balance on one foot, you can change.

Take all you learned from those mistakes and make that a springboard to propel you further in life, towards new goals. No matter how perfect you think everyone else is, no one has a perfect life. If you dwell on the past, there will be no time to enjoy the present or plan for the future. I know I told you that this wasn't some cheesy self-help book, but, on the other hand, those cheesy self-help books make a lot of good points. So here goes mine, I think. You might not be able to change your situation, but you can always change the way you look at it and deal with it.

"Success is how high you bounce after you hit bottom." – General George Patton

CHRISTOPHER GRANT

ATYCHIPHOBIA

Failure is what success eats for breakfast.

This book is filled with scary thoughts and ideas - fears that we all have or had - as wantrepreneurs. The other F-word I love is failure. The fear of failure is called atychiphobia. If you think you are alone in suffering from atychiphobia, you are not. So many people put off achieving their dreams or goals because they fear that they will fail. I don't know any scientific numbers or figures about the number of people, who never try because they don't want to fail, because, well, they never tried.

If you start a business, you have achieved so much more than everyone else in the world, who thought about it, but never took the steps to do it. That is one very big "if". Starting a business is great, but you also need the drive to see it through. Like any great road trip, starting the car is the easy part. Once started, you can either let it run in the driveway, or you can go somewhere. I would recommend you go somewhere.

When I started out, I had the fear that if my business

failed, everyone would see it crumble and watch me walk away like in some epic movie ending. In reality, my first business did fail. I started it, ran it, grew it, and saw it fail, all within six years. How did I fail? I didn't like working anymore.

The greenhouse company I owned became boring, monotonous, and daunting. On paper, the business was surviving. In real life, it consumed me. It became work. The business was a success, but I thought I had failed. I would make up these elaborate images of what people thought about me - my suppliers, customers, competition, friends, and family. I had to finally shut all of that nonsense out and remember that I was the only person to worry about.

Today, they see me with my new business, a fun business that I love. I could have wrapped up my greenhouse business and gone on to occupy a cubicle, but I didn't. I took all of the lessons I learned from running that business, at such a young age, and rolled them into my next business. I like to think that Grant's Plants was the first step in forming Grant Family Farm. Did I fail? Yes, yes I did. Did I give up? Hell, no. I knew that I had a business in me. It just took a while for it to come out.

"Fearlessness is like a muscle. I know from my own life that the more I exercise it the more natural it becomes to not let my fears run me."
— Arianna Huffington

Countless businesses have started up, and flopped for one reason or another. That is nothing to laugh at or get you down, it is just a fact that nothing lasts forever. I am not going to slap a statistic here with failure rates. Making a mistake when your business is small will cost you time and money, but you can find a way to get back on track, even if you think the end is near.

Large organizations fail endeavors, but can survive because of the scale they are working with. I recently came across a post on Facebook, of all places, that showed a collection of abandoned places around the world, and two of them were Disney Parks! Disney's Discovery Island and Disney's River Country were built to be the next big thing in Disney theme park entertainment, but are now abandoned.

The location has been trespassed on by those with cameras, who then leak pictures and videos of the parks that once attracted families from around the world, but which are now lying in a deserted, post-apocalyptic state. If you think of all the moving parts that make up the Disney Corporation, these two parks were only a drop in the bucket, and when they were losing popularity for one reason or another, they gave up on them to focus on what worked. All the infrastructure and engineering that went into the parks just left behind, and they moved on to create the next big thing for the business.

Do you think Disney learned from these two failed

endeavors? I think so. You also have to think about all of the projects that were developed by a company like Disney and never made it past the table model. However you feel about the Disney business model, you have to admire one thing about them, the ability to keep moving forward during so many difficult periods of history. Disney is so successful because they have stuck to the same philosophy all these years; they "create happiness" and "make magic happen." Disney continues to be a leader in entertainment because of just that, even though not every endeavor they dream up can survive on happiness and magic.

"There is only one thing that makes a dream impossible to achieve: the fear of failure."
— Paulo Coelho

Beyond business, you have your own priorities in life. You are faced with an opportunity to take a chance and do something that is different, do something that no one else does, and you can look at it one of two ways. You can take a leap of faith, do something "crazy," and find small failures until you succeed. When you succeed you are no longer categorized as "crazy" but a "visionary."

The other option is to look at the opportunity and then compromise, or shoot lower because you don't want to be "different" or "crazy" or anything else but normal. I have always been that "different" or "crazy" person in the crowd because I owned a business when everyone else was in college, jumping from part-time job to part-time job.

There comes a time where you cannot fear being wrong; you cannot fear making mistakes in both life and business. If you follow your gut and play the cards that are dealt to you, success is inevitable. If you go after it, will you fail? Like the Dr. Seuss book, *Oh, the Places You Will Go*, you may fail until you succeed, but end with: "And will you succeed? Yes! You will, indeed! 98 and ¾ percent guaranteed." Not bad odds coming from this timeless children's book.

> *"Success consists of going from failure to failure without loss of enthusiasm."*
> — Winston Churchill

THE HONEST TRUTH

Here it is again. Here is the honest truth. If you work forty hours per week from age 25 to age 65, you will work roughly 83,200 hours. This is assuming you work five days a week with some vacation time factored in. If you break it down, that is equal to about 9.5 years of your life. In reality, you will probably work some overtime and, in this day in age, it is unlikely you will retire completely at age 65. I will be conservative and call it 10 years. I already said that.

If you are going to have to work for 10 years in order to survive, feed your family, and achieve the kind of lifestyle you want, you might as well enjoy your job. It is a crazy idea to think that if you had to do anything for ten solid years, you would do something boring. If I had to work for ten solid years in a job that I didn't love, what would it be for? Unfortunately the ten years we will work are spread out over 40-plus years in the work force. I am sure that you know someone who hates their job. Maybe it's you. Maybe you work at a job that pays the bills, but that's all.

When you are on the edge, thinking about starting a business and following your dreams, failure, being inadequate, timing, money, what other people will think, distractions, mistakes, changing visions, and failure all stand in your way and hold you back. These all look harmless on paper, so go ahead, and write them down. Then laugh at them. When it comes to reality, these fears are legitimate. These fears are relevant to every aspect of your life. They keep you awake at night, distract you from your task at hand, and even make you sick. You could fear failing a test, bouncing a check, waking up late, or missing a chance to do something amazing. If you think I'm crazy, that's OK.

Because each day, I wake up and have a job that I love to go to. I get to grow good food for people. When I started at the age of 16, I conquered these fears, and I work hard to overcome them every day. If I could jump off the page and tell you one thing, it is this: if you want to do something amazing, to change your life and the lives of the people around you, to make the world a little better, and to love your job, **start now**.

Is it a romantic idea to be able to do what you love? Yes, but with all of the negativity in the world, you should take your energy and make something good, something worthwhile, and something that you can be proud of. The average life expectancy in America hovers around eighty years. If you have to work ten years straight, maybe more, you might as well do something that makes you happy every day.

If your business fails, congratulations. Although it may be painful at first, know that you have just accomplished something that so many people in this world have dreamt about, but never took the first step in starting. With that first failure behind you, don't stop trying. If you choose to get a job in between ventures, your resume will shine because you were bold enough to start a business and you know just how hard it is to stay afloat. You are now incredibly valuable to other businesses. If you are running your business now, keep moving forward, and be true to your values. Never stop entrepreneuring.

For every wantrepreneur reading this, I am sure that you may have rolled your eyes once or twice in the process. You might think that you already knew everything that you read. The best piece of advice I can give to you is to start. Start right now. After you put this book down I hope you pick up a pen and write. I started on a single post-it note. Start playing the game. Take chances, risk boldly, and try something. Because if you are just along for the ride, the journey you take will be up to the driver of the bus. We are only here for a short period of time, and time is one commodity you can't buy more of. Never take tomorrow for granted. You will be amazed by just how much you can accomplish when you write down all the reasons that are holding you back and why you shouldn't start. Then on a new piece of paper, write down all the reasons you should go for it, all you could gain and achieve by starting your dream business. I hope the second list you make will outweigh the first.

I want to point out that I haven't cited any scary statistics about business failure rates thus far. The kind of statistics that college professors throw at students to scare them into mediocrity. Don't worry, now is not the time either. Like I said earlier, now is the time to change the way you think. Start thinking like an entrepreneur. Don't worry about falling into the failure statistics, but strive to be one of those who make up the business success statistics.

"Great minds think alike, great entrepreneurs do not."
   - Chris Grant

They say that great minds think alike. That may be true, but great entrepreneurs do not. Great entrepreneurs think like no one else. If you can forget about sitting in rows of students, thinking that you can only thrive in this life if you are at the top of your class, and thinking that this dream or that dream is out of reach, and throw all that out the window, then you can be an entrepreneur.

Now is the time to blaze your own trail. There is no such thing as normal in this crazy world that we live in. If you want to have an adventure and to live outside the box, now is the time to take that step. Don't try to forget or ignore the fears that arise, as you think about taking the leap into business. Embrace each fear as an opportunity to grow (once again, no pun intended). When the day comes that you get your business cards in the mail, your first customer, and the first dollar that you can tape on the wall, enjoy it, because you overcame all of the fears of a wantrepreneur, and became a full-fledged entrepreneur.

"Twenty years from now you will be more disappointed by the things that you didn't do than by the ones you did do. So throw off the bowlines. Sail away from the safe harbor. Catch the trade winds in your sails. Explore. Dream. Discover."
- H. Jackson Brown, Jr.

Is it scary to think that one day you could be your own boss? Yes, it is scary. But it is not so scary that you shouldn't at least take a chance. I think it is scarier to think about all the times I should have taken a risk and gone for something, but never did. Good things come to those who wait. That may be true, but great things only come to those who go out and get them.

Go get them.

A special dedication to Rob –

Never again will I take the gift of today for granted

Made in the USA
San Bernardino, CA
24 April 2014